MATH
By All Means®

DIVISION
Grades 3–4

MATH
By All Means®

DIVISION
Grades 3–4

by Susan Ohanian
and Marilyn Burns

A MARILYN BURNS REPLACEMENT UNIT

MATH SOLUTIONS PUBLICATIONS

Editorial direction: Lorri Ungaretti
Art direction and design: Aileen Friedman
Typesetting: Rad H. M. Proctor
Page makeup: David Healy, First Image
Illustrations: David Healy, First Image
Cover background and border designs: Barbara Gelfand

Marilyn Burns Education Associates is dedicated to improving mathematics education. For information about Math Solutions courses, resource materials, and other services, write or call:

Marilyn Burns Education Associates
150 Gate 5 Road, Suite 101
Sausalito, CA 94965
Telephone (415) 332-4181 or (800) 868-9092
Fax (415) 331-1931

ISBN 0-941355-06-3

This book is printed on recycled paper.

Distributed by Cuisenaire Company of America, Inc.
P.O. Box 5026
White Plains, NY 10602-5026
(800) 237-3142

PREFACE

This unit was first created by Bonnie Tank and me in the 1989–90 school year and tested by 8 teachers in the San Francisco Bay Area and 24 teachers in Tucson Unified School District Chapter 1 schools. In January 1993, Lynne Zolli, one of the teachers who had originally tested the unit, taught the unit for the fourth time. Susan Ohanian attended her class daily to observe and take notes.

I've long admired Susan's educational writing and was thrilled that she was willing to tackle this project. Not only would she bring her clear, thoughtful, and experienced view of education to a *Math By All Means* unit, but she would also help me see the unit from her perspective as an educator not directly connected to my work on the mathematics curriculum.

Susan stayed as a guest at my home that month, her home being in Schenectady, New York. She returned from school each day with a fistful of student work that we pored over and discussed. I had taught the unit twice previously, and it was fascinating for me not only to see another set of children's work but also to learn how Lynne structured some of the activities. From time to time, Susan, Lynne, and I met to talk about what we noticed or to discuss new ideas to try.

Susan returned home at the end of January and spent the next several months writing the manuscript. In the meantime, Lynne continued the unit with a few more activities and sent additional student work to Susan. By late spring, Susan had completed the first draft.

What amazed Lynne when she read the draft was that Susan clearly had a different perspective on the class. Not having the responsibility of teaching, Susan focused primarily on how the children reacted and what they did. Lynne's focus in the classroom was on teaching the lessons, managing the class, and encouraging, prodding, and helping students as needed. When Lynne read Susan's manuscript, she gained new perceptions, seeing children from Susan's position at the back of the room. Lynne's reaction reminded me how focused we are as teachers and how difficult it is to be aware of what each child in a room of 30 children is doing at all times.

My contribution to the manuscript was to add to each lesson insights from Lynne's point of view. To do this, I talked extensively with Lynne, drew upon what I had done when I taught the unit, and enlisted the help of education student Leyani von Rotz. In 1994, one year after Susan's observation, Lynne again taught the division unit, and Leyani observed the class as part of her teacher education program. She took notes from a front-of-the-room perspective.

When I completed my work, Lynne again read and responded to the manuscript. We refined some lessons, added a new lesson that we had begun to discuss when Susan was observing, and talked about what we had learned and what we would change. We agreed that we were pleased with the unit and ready to send it off for production into a book.

So, here it is. This book is testimony to the benefit of cooperative work. As you might expect, this unit on division changed and evolved during the two years we were writing it, as well as over the five years teachers have tested it. I suspect that teachers will continue to find ways to do things differently to make sense of the unit for them and their students. As always, I am interested in your feedback.

Marilyn Burns
October 1994

Acknowledgments

Special thanks to Lynne Zolli, a teacher at Jefferson School in San Francisco, California. Lynne opened her classroom to our scrutiny, saved every scrap of children's work, read the manuscript in several drafts, and was always available to discuss our questions. Her support contributed enormously to this book.

We also appreciate the contribution of Leyani von Rotz, who, as part of her teacher education program at Mills College in Oakland, California, observed Lynne Zolli's class, took copious notes, and translated those notes into a collection of extremely useful descriptions.

In addition, we appreciate the help of Joanne Lewin, another teacher at Jefferson School, for trying activities with her class and sharing her experiences with us.

CONTENTS

Introduction   1

Assessments   13

    What Is Division?   15
    What Is 20 ÷ 4?   105
    Classroom Groups   125
    Four Ways to Solve 21 ÷ 4   152
    Explaining 13 ÷ 4 = 3 R1   174
    How Are Division and
        Multiplication Alike?   180

Whole Class Lessons   21

    Sharing Money   22
    The Doorbell Rang   32
    Dividing Cookies   49
    The Game of Leftovers   60
    Explorations with Raisins   72

Menu Activities   83

    The Doorbell Rings Again   89
    Leftovers with Any Number   95
    Raisins in the Big Box   109
    Candy Box Family Guides   116
    17 Kings and 42 Elephants   135
    Sharing Candy Bars   145
    Hungry Ants   157
    Division Stories   167

Children's Books   **185**

The Doorbell Rang	186
One Hundred Hungry Ants	186
17 Kings and 42 Elephants	187

Homework   **189**

Dividing with Two People	190
Leftovers	190
A Sharing Problem	191
A Grouping Problem	192

Blackline Masters   **193**

Division Menu	194
Dividing Cookies (recording sheet)	195
Cookies (recording sheet)	196
Directions for Playing Leftovers	197–198
The Doorbell Rings Again	199
Leftovers with Any Number	200
Raisins in the Big Box	201
Candy Box Family Guides	202
17 Kings and 42 Elephants	203
Sharing Candy Bars	204
Candy Bars (recording sheet)	205
Hungry Ants	206
Division Stories	207

Bibliography   **209**

Index   **211**

INTRODUCTION

After reading aloud the children's book *17 Kings and 42 Elephants*, Lynne Zolli gave her students the problem of figuring out how 17 kings could equally share the responsibility of caring for 42 elephants. Lynne introduced this as a menu activity, when the class was several weeks into the unit. Children's responses revealed the different ways they approached finding a solution to $42 \div 17$ and showed that they typically relied on what they knew about the other operations—addition, subtraction, and multiplication—to solve division problems.

Truc, for example, estimated that each king would have to take care of 2 elephants, then added 17 2s to find out how many elephants that accounted for.

Brittany, however, used subtraction, first subtracting 17 from 42 to get 25, then subtracting 17 again to get 8.

Gabrielle used both addition and subtraction. She added 17 and 17 to get 34, then added 17 again to get 51 and wrote: *If you gave each king three elephants it would be too much.* She then subtracted 34 from 42 and reported: *Each king will get two elephants. And eight elephants is left over.*

Matthew found a way to use multiplication to solve the problem. First he estimated and wrote: *Each king will get about 2 elephants to take care of.* Then he multiplied and wrote: *Since 2 × 17 makes 34 there will be 8 left over.*

Even though these children used different operations, they all reported that the answer to $42 \div 17$ was 2 with a remainder of 8.

Several other children tried to solve the same problem by using a calculator to divide 42 by 17. However, they abandoned this strategy when they weren't able to interpret 2.4705882 in the context of 17 kings sharing the responsibility for 42 elephants.

In this unit, students are given a broad range of problem-solving experiences with division. They learn to identify the wide variety of situations that relate to division. They learn how to represent division problems symbolically and explore different options for dealing with remainders. Throughout the unit, children are free to use calculators; however, they must be able to explain the answer in order for it to be an acceptable solution. The focus of the unit is on making division meaningful rather than a mechanical procedure.

Teaching Division in the Elementary Grades

Children informally use division long before they receive any formal instruction. Their early experiences are with two different types of division. One is when they share objects, such as dividing 20 marbles among four friends and seeing that each person gets 5 marbles; the second is when they divide a number of objects into equal-size groups, such as cutting out 20 paper petals, gluing 4 petals to a flower, and seeing how many flowers they have.

For the first type of division, *sharing* or *partitioning*, children usually divide objects by doling them out, one by one, until there aren't any more or there aren't enough for another round. For example, if they want to share 20 marbles among four children, they can give them out, one by one, until each child has 5 marbles. Similarly, when organizing a class of 28 students into two teams, children usually assign players one at a time, first to one team and then to the other, ultimately dividing the class into two groups with 14 children in each. In sharing situations, the *size of the total amount* and the *number of shares* are known; what's unknown is the *size of each share.* In a real situation, children can solve the problem concretely. Solving the problem numerically, however, calls for an understanding of multiplication that allows children to answer the question, "Four times what number equals 20?" or, "Two times what number equals 28?"

The other interpretation of division, called *grouping,* calls for splitting a number into equal-size groups. For example, using 20 paper petals to make flowers with 4 petals on each calls for gluing the petals in groups of 4. Organizing a class of 28 students into pairs involves forming groups of 2 until all children have been accounted for. As in sharing situations, the *size of the total amount* is known. However, also known is the *size of each group* and the unknown is the *number of groups.*

The word *division* is used for both sharing and grouping problems, and both kinds of problems are represented the same way numerically. However, each type is interpreted differently. Both of the classroom examples above can be recorded as:

$$28 \div 2 = 14 \text{ or } 2\overline{)28}^{14}$$

In the sharing situation, 14 is the result of "28 students divided into two groups"; in the grouping situation, 14 is the result of "28 students divided into groups of 2."

Children's initial experiences with division should be with both types. Students' power with division increases when they begin to understand the connection between sharing and grouping and can connect both types of division with the other operations of addition, subtraction, and multiplication.

Concentrating instruction on teaching children the algorithm for calculating answers to all division problems is not only a narrow approach to division instruction, but also runs the risk of misrepresenting division as an operation with a unilateral interpretation. Classroom instruction should focus on giving children a variety of division problems of both types to solve, with and without remainders, helping them both to relate sharing to grouping and to use their knowledge of the other number operations to explore both types of division. The goal of instruction is to uncover the idea of division in its full complexity, not to cover the idea from a view toward algorithmic proficiency.

What's in the Unit?

In this five-week unit, students are given a broad range of problem-solving experiences with division. To integrate division with the rest of mathematics, the activities include ideas from the strands of number, geometry, statistics, and patterns. Also, the unit assumes that the children have already learned about multiplication before studying this unit on division.

During the unit, children participate in whole class lessons, work cooperatively in pairs and small groups, and complete individual assignments. Writing is an integral part of their math learning, and children's books are incorporated into the lessons. Homework further enhances the classroom experiences and communicates with parents about their child's learning.

A challenge of teaching is to find activities that capture children's imaginations, give them access to a mathematical idea such as division, and allow them to construct their own understanding of that idea. Not all children respond with the same interest to the same activities or learn equally well from them. Because of this, the unit provides a range of activities to help children find their own ways to learn.

All of the students in the class do the same activities. The activities are designed to be accessible for students with limited experience and understanding while, at the same time, to be of interest and value to students with more experience and deeper understanding. Throughout the unit, students develop understanding from interactions with the teacher, conversations with other students, opportunities to work with concrete materials, and problems that make them think about numbers.

The Structure of This Book

The directions for instruction in this unit are organized into five components: *Whole Class Lessons, Menu Activities, Assessments, Children's Books*, and *Homework*. Blackline masters needed for the activities, as well as a bibliography, are included.

Whole Class Lessons

Five whole class lessons are suggested for the unit. In the first lesson, children are introduced to division through a real-world topic of great interest to them—money. In the second lesson, children share cookies and use the conventional symbolism of division. The third lesson also engages the children with sharing cookies, this time introducing them to fractional parts as well. In the fourth lesson, children learn to play a game that focuses their attention on remainders in division problems. The fifth lesson involves children with estimating, statistical reasoning, and whole-number operations as they try to share raisins equally.

The instructional directions for each lesson are presented in four sections:

Overview gives a brief description of the lesson.

Before the lesson outlines the preparation needed before teaching the lesson.

Teaching directions gives step-by-step instructions for presenting the lesson.

From the Classroom describes what happened when the lesson was taught in an actual classroom. The vignette helps bring alive the instructional guidelines by giving an over-the-shoulder look into a classroom, telling how lessons were organized, how students reacted, and how the teacher responded. The vignettes are not standards of what "should" happen, but a record of what did happen with a class of children.

Menu Activities

The menu is a collection of activities that children do independently—in pairs, groups, or individually. The tasks on the menu give children a variety of experiences with division but do not conceptually build on one another and, therefore, are not meant to be done in any particular sequence. Rather, menu activities pose problems, set up situations, and ask questions that help students interact with division in a variety of ways. There are eight activities on the menu, three of which extend whole class lessons and five that present new experiences.

The instructional directions for each menu activity are presented in four sections:

Overview gives a brief description of the lesson.

Before the lesson outlines the preparation needed before teaching the lesson.

Getting started gives instructions for introducing the activity.

From the Classroom describes what happened when the activity was introduced in a classroom. As with the whole class lessons, the vignette gives a view into an actual classroom, describing how the teacher gave directions and how the students responded.

For additional information about using menus, see the introduction to the Menu Activities section that begins on page 83.

Assessments

Assessing what children understand is a continual process. Teachers learn what their students know from listening to what the children report in class discussions, from observing and listening to them as they work on independent activities, and from reading their written work. Because not all children contribute to class discussions, and students usually work collaboratively in class, it's useful to assess children periodically with assignments that they complete individually and in writing.

Such assessments are no different in character from instructional activities. They are opportunities for children to continue their learning about division; they also give the teacher specific information about what individual children understand.

This unit suggests six assessments. One is suggested for the beginning of the unit and the rest are sprinkled throughout to help teachers monitor students' progress. The assessments are listed in the Table of Contents and are identified within the unit by gray bars in the margins.

For specific information about assessing understanding, see the introduction to the Assessments section on page 13.

Children's Books

Children's books can be a motivating way to engage children in mathematical thinking and reasoning. They also provide a way to integrate literature with math instruction. For this unit, we recommend three children's books. One is used for both a whole class lesson and a menu activity, and the other two form the basis of menu activities. The Children's Books section includes a synopsis of each book and references for where the book is used in the unit.

Homework

Homework assignments have two purposes: They extend the work children are doing in class, and they inform parents about the instruction their children are getting. Suggestions for homework assignments and ways to communicate with parents are included in the Homework section.

Blackline Masters

Blackline masters are provided for all menu activities and recording sheets.

Bibliography

A bibliography of resources cited in the unit appears on page 209.

Notes About Classroom Organization

Setting the Stage for Cooperation

Throughout much of the unit, students work cooperatively with partners or in small groups. Interaction is an important ingredient for children's intellec-

tual development. They learn from interaction with one another as well as with adults.

Teachers who have taught this unit report different systems for organizing children to work cooperatively. Some put pairs of numbers in a bag and have children draw to choose partners. Some assign partners or groups. Some have seatmates work together. Others let children pick their own partners. Some teachers have students work with the same partner for the entire unit. Others let children choose partners for each activity, allowing them either to change frequently or stay with the same person. Some don't have children work with specific partners but instead with others who have chosen the same activity.

The system for organizing children matters less than the underlying classroom attitude. What's important is that children are encouraged to work together, listen to one another's ideas, and be willing to help classmates. Students should see their classroom as a place where cooperation and collaboration are valued and expected. This does not mean, of course, that children are never expected to work individually. However, it does respect the principle that interaction fosters learning and, therefore, that cooperation is basic to the culture of the classroom.

A System for the Menu Activities

Teachers report different ways of organizing the menu activities. Some teachers use a copy machine to enlarge the blackline masters of the menu tasks onto 11-by-17-inch paper, mount them on construction paper or tagboard, and post them. Although children are introduced orally to each activity, later they can refer to the directions for clarification. (Note: A set of posters with the menu activities is available for purchase from Cuisenaire Company of America.)

Rather than enlarge and post the tasks, other teachers duplicate about a half dozen of each and make them available for children to take to their seats. Some teachers also mount the tasks on tagboard to make the copies more durable. And other teachers put the tasks in booklets, making one booklet for each child or pair of students.

For each of the above alternatives, children take materials from the general supply and return them when they finish their work or at the end of class.

Each of these systems encourages children to be independent and responsible for their learning. Children are allowed to spend the amount of time needed on any one activity and to make choices about the sequence in which they work on tasks.

How Children Record

Teachers also use different procedures to organize the way children record. Some prepare folders for each child, either by folding 12-by-18-inch sheets of construction paper or by using regular file folders, and require children to record individually even when working cooperatively. Some teachers prepare folders for partners and have the partners collaborate on their written work. Other teachers don't use folders but have students place their finished work in an In basket.

Some teachers have children copy the list of menu activities and keep track of what they do by putting a check by an activity each time they do it. Other teachers give children a list of the menu activities by duplicating the blackline master on page 194. It's important that the recording system is clear to the class and helps the teacher keep track of children's progress.

About Writing in Math Class

For both learning activities and assessments, teachers must rely on children's writing to get insights into their thinking. Helping children learn to describe their reasoning processes, and become comfortable doing so, is extremely important and requires planning and attention. Experience and encouragement are two major ingredients.

It's important for children to know that their writing is important because it helps the teacher learn about how they are reasoning. Teachers need to reinforce over and over again that the teacher is the audience for children's writing; therefore, the students need to provide sufficient details to make their thinking and reasoning processes clear.

Managing Materials and Supplies

Teachers who have taught this unit gave children time to explore the concrete materials they needed to use. Most teachers devoted several weeks at the beginning of the school year to free exploration of materials. Also, all teachers gave students guidelines for the care and storage of materials. The following materials and supplies are needed for this unit:

Materials

- Color Tiles (1-inch square tiles in four colors), one set of 400
- Dice, about one die per child
- Blank cubes and labels for making dice, about one per child
- Raisins, $\frac{1}{2}$-ounce boxes, one per child
- Raisins, $1\frac{1}{2}$-ounce boxes, one per group of four students
- Play money (optional)
- Paper cups or other small containers

General Classroom Supplies

- Ample supplies of paper, including large sheets of newsprint or chart paper and 12-by-18-inch paper
- Small paper plates, six for each pair of children (3-inch squares of construction paper can be substituted)
- Scissors, at least one for each pair of children
- Glue or tape

In addition, recording sheets specified for individual activities are included in the Blackline Masters section. Most teachers choose to have supplies of each sheet available for children to take when needed. Also, see the Children's Books section on page 185 for information about the children's books that have been integrated into this unit.

A Comment About Calculators

It is assumed that during this unit, and in the classroom throughout the year, calculators are as available to the children as pencils, paper, rulers, and other general classroom supplies. You may occasionally ask students not to use calculators if you want to know about their ability to work with numbers on their own. However, such times should be the exception rather than the rule. Children should regard calculators as tools that are generally available for their use when doing mathematics.

As with other materials, children need time to become familiar with calculators. Some children will find them fascinating and useful; others will not be interested in or comfortable with them.

A Suggested Daily Schedule

It's helpful to think through the entire unit and make an overall teaching plan. However, it isn't possible to predict how a class will respond as the unit progresses, and adjustments and changes will most likely have to be made. The following day-to-day schedule is a suggested five-week guide. It offers a plan that varies the pace of daily instruction, interweaving days for whole class lessons with days for independent work on menu activities. The schedule also suggests times for discussing menu activities and giving homework assignments.

Class discussions of menu activities are included throughout the day-to-day plan. These are typically scheduled several days or more after the menu activity is introduced, giving children time to experience the activity before being asked to participate in a class discussion. Since students will be working on menu activities at their own pace and completing them at different times, it's important to check with children about their progress. At times, you might mention to children that they'll be discussing a particular activity the next day and should be sure to work on the task so they can all contribute to the discussion. Although times for class discussions are suggested in the plan, use your judgment about when it's best to have them. For suggestions about how to conduct class discussions, check the "From the Classroom" section in each menu activity.

Day 1   **Assessment: What Is Division?**

Talk about division with the children. Ask them to work in small groups and write about what they know.

Day 2   **Whole Class Lesson: Sharing Money**

Introduce the lesson. Have children figure out how to share $5.00, and then 50 cents, among four people.

Day 3   **Whole Class Lesson: The Doorbell Rang**

Read and discuss the book *The Doorbell Rang.* Explain to children how to summarize the story using mathematical symbolism and then to write an additional event. The children begin work on the assignment.

Day 4   **Whole Class Lesson: The Doorbell Rang (continued)**

Review the book *The Doorbell Rang* and let students continue working on their stories. Give homework assignment: *Dividing with Two People.*

Day 5   **Whole Class Lesson: The Doorbell Rang (continued)**

Begin class by having students compare their solutions to the homework assignment *Dividing with Two People.* Then initiate a class discussion in which children present the events they added to *The Doorbell Rang.*

Day 6   **Whole Class Lesson: Dividing Cookies**

Introduce the lesson and have children work in groups to divide six, five, three, two, and one cookie among four people.

Day 7   **Whole Class Lesson: The Game of Leftovers**

Introduce the game of Leftovers. Have children play with partners and record on a class chart statements with remainders of zero.

Day 8   **Whole Class Lesson: The Game of Leftovers (continued)**

The children continue playing Leftovers. Discuss the statements they've recorded on the class chart.

Day 9   **Introduce Menu Activities: The Doorbell Rings Again, Leftovers with Any Number**

Present the directions for the menu activities *The Doorbell Rings Again* and *Leftovers with Any Number.* Students choose activities to work on for the remainder of the class.

Day 10   **Menu**

Students work on menu activities. Give homework assignment: *Leftovers.*

Day 11 **Assessment: What Is 20 ÷ 4?**

Begin class by having students report their experiences playing Leftovers at home. Then present the *What Is 20 ÷ 4?* assessment. When children complete the assessment, they choose menu activities to work on for the remainder of the class.

Day 12 **Whole Class Lesson: Explorations with Raisins**

Introduce the lesson. Children estimate the number of raisins in a ¹/₂-ounce box, count them, and then work in groups to divide the raisins equally.

Day 13 **Introduce Menu Activities: Raisins in the Big Box, Candy Box Family Guides**

Begin class by having a few children share their stories from *The Doorbell Rings Again.* Then collect class data for the "Family Sizes in Our Class" chart. Use this information to introduce the menu activity *Candy Box Family Guides.* Also present the directions for the menu activity *Raisins in the Big Box.* Students choose activities to work on for the remainder of the class.

Day 14 **Menu**

Begin class with a class discussion about Leftovers and also with a few children sharing their stories from *The Doorbell Rings Again.* Then students work on menu activities.

Day 15 **Assessment: Classroom Groups**

Present the *Classroom Groups* assessment. When children complete the assessment, they choose menu activities to work on for the remainder of the class.

Day 16 **Introduce Menu Activity: 17 Kings and 42 Elephants**

Begin class by discussing children's results from the menu activity *Raisins in the Big Box.* Then read and discuss the book *17 Kings and 42 Elephants* and introduce the menu activity. Give homework assignment: *A Sharing Problem.*

Day 17 **Menu**

Begin class by having students discuss their solutions to the homework assignment *A Sharing Problem.* Then students work on menu activities. Tell the class to be ready tomorrow to discuss the *Candy Box Family Guides* menu activity.

Day 18 **Introduce Menu Activity: Sharing Candy Bars**

Begin class by discussing the mathematics of the *Candy Box Family Guides* menu activity. Then introduce the menu activity *Sharing Candy Bars.* Students choose menu activities to work on for the remainder of the class. Tell them to be ready tomorrow to discuss their solutions for the *17 Kings and 42 Elephants* menu activity.

Day 19 Menu

Begin class by discussing the students' solutions for the *17 Kings and 42 Elephants* menu activity. Then students choose menu activities to work on for the remainder of the class.

Day 20 Assessment: Four Ways to Solve 21 ÷ 4

Present the *Four Ways to Solve 21 ÷ 4* assessment. After children complete the assessment, they choose menu activities to work on for the remainder of the class. Tell children to be ready tomorrow to discuss *Sharing Candy Bars.*

Day 21 Introduce Menu Activity: Hungry Ants

Begin class by discussing the students' solutions for the *Sharing Candy Bars* menu activity. Then read the book *One Hundred Hungry Ants* and introduce the menu activity *Hungry Ants.* Students choose menu activities to work on for the remainder of the class.

Day 22 Introduce Menu Activity: Division Stories

Introduce the menu activity *Division Stories.* Students choose menu activities to work on for the remainder of the class. Give them the homework assignment: *A Grouping Problem.*

Day 23 Menu

Begin class with students comparing their solutions to the homework assignment *A Grouping Problem.* Then students work on menu activities.

Day 24 Assessment: Explaining 13 ÷ 4 = 3 R1

Present the *Explaining 13 ÷ 4 = 3 R1* assessment. After children complete the assessment, they choose menu activities to work on for the remainder of the class. Tell them to be ready tomorrow to discuss work from the *Hungry Ants* menu activity.

Day 25 Assessment: How Are Division and Multiplication Alike?

Begin class by discussing the students' work from the *Hungry Ants* menu activity. Then present the *How Are Division and Multiplication Alike?* assessment.

A Letter to Parents

Although parents learn about their child's experiences from homework assignments and papers sent home, you may want to give them general information about the unit before you begin teaching it. The following is a sample letter that informs parents about the goals of the unit and introduces them to some of the activities their child will be doing.

Dear Parent,

In our next math unit, the children learn about division, a standard topic in the elementary mathematics curriculum. The unit involves the children with division in a variety of ways: The children solve problems, explore with concrete materials, write story problems about division, and play games that help them learn about division and the symbolism used to represent it.

The unit engages the children by relating division to the world around them. They investigate how to share cookies, raisins, and money among several different size groups. Through these experiences, they are introduced to the standard mathematical symbolism for division. They also learn a game called Leftovers, which gives them experience representing remainders and investigating numerical patterns. And they are introduced to three children's books that can be used for problem-solving experiences with division.

The emphasis of the unit is on helping children understand the concept of division and solve problems in ways that make sense to them. Our classroom instruction focuses on making division meaningful rather than mechanical.

Please feel welcome to visit the class at any time.

Sincerely,

A Final Comment

The decisions teachers make every day in the classroom are the heart of teaching. Although this book attempts to provide clear and detailed information about lessons and activities, it is not a recipe that can be followed step by step. Rather, the book offers options that require teachers to make decisions in several areas: sequencing activities, organizing the classroom, grouping children, communicating with parents, and meeting the needs of individual children. Keep in mind that there is no "best" or "right" way to teach the unit. The aim is to engage children in mathematical investigations, inspire them to think and reason, and enable them to enjoy their learning.

CONTENTS

What Is Division?   15
What Is 20 ÷ 4?   105
Classroom Groups   125
Four Ways to Solve 21 ÷ 4   152
Explaining 13 ÷ 4 = 3 R1   174
How Are Division and Multiplication Alike? 180

ASSESSMENTS

Assessing children's understanding is an ongoing process. In the classroom, teachers learn about what students know from listening to what they say during class discussions, observing and listening as students work on independent activities, conversing with individual students, and reading students' written work. From these observations and interactions, teachers gain insights into their students' thinking and reasoning processes and learn about their students' mathematical interests and abilities.

Typically, division instruction focuses on facts and computation, and assessment is concerned with whether children can "do" division. Teachers test students on their knowledge of division facts and their ability to compute by using the standard algorithm. Students are asked to solve mostly one-step word problems.

The focus of this unit is much different. The activities give children experience with division in several mathematical contexts. Students examine patterns, work with rectangular arrays, analyze statistical data, solve problems with money, and use division in real-world contexts. They learn the standard symbolism and solve problems that require them to use division facts. They encounter problems with and without remainders. They use a variety of manipulative materials. Their numerical calculations are not isolated, but are embedded in broader mathematical settings.

Six assessments are suggested. *What Is Division?* given at the start of the unit, helps identify what children know about division. In *What Is 20 ÷ 4?* students explain division to an imaginary classmate, revealing how well they understand the basic idea and symbolism of division. *Classroom Groups* shows whether children can solve division problems in a real-life context. *Four Ways to Solve 21 ÷ 4* asks students to solve the same numerical division problem in four different contexts, presenting the problem of looking at remainders in different ways, depending on the context.

Explaining 13 ÷ 4 = 3 R1 is similar to *What Is 20 ÷ 4?* providing another assessment later in the unit. In *How Are Division and Multiplication Alike?* students explain their understanding of how division and multiplication relate to each other.

These assessments are essentially no different from some of the menu activities in which students solve problems or relate division to real-world situations. However, in the assessments, students work individually so that the teacher has the opportunity to gain insights into how each child thinks.

ASSESSMENT What Is Division?

FROM THE CLASSROOM

Many children have some familiarity with division before they receive formal instruction in the classroom. They have heard about division from parents, from older brothers and sisters, or at day care. Even with prior experience, however, most children do not have a comprehensive understanding of what division is or how to use it.

Begin an initial assessment with a class discussion. Tell the children that you're interested in hearing what they know about division. Hear from all volunteers, accepting their thoughts without judgment or correction. You may want to ask children to clarify their ideas, but don't push too hard. This is not a time to teach but, rather, to collect information about the range of understanding and experience in the class.

After all interested students have responded, ask the students to talk in small groups about what they know about division. Then have them collaborate to write down their ideas about what division means and the kinds of things that can be divided. The students' writing will give you further information about their perceptions.

Lynne introduced the unit by gathering her class of 30 students on the floor at the front of the room and asking, "When I say the word *divide,* what do you think of?"

A half dozen children raised their hands, eager to answer. Lynne waited, giving more children a chance to think about the question before she called on anyone. Then she had all who were interested offer their ideas.

"Pizza," said Ashley.

"How does pizza make you think of division?" Lynne asked.

"When you cut it, you divide it up," Ashley answered.

"Divide is a line and a dot on top and bottom," Ethan offered next.

"Show us what you mean," prompted Lynne, inviting Ethan to come to the board. He wrote: ÷.

Other children murmured, "Oh, yeah." "I've seen that." "I remember."

Lynne then called on Hugh.

"Dividing things, make sure it's even," he said.

"What do you mean by *even?*" Lynne asked him.

"If you had a square, you could cut it in half," explained Hugh. "Can I come up and show?" Lynne nodded, and Hugh came to the board, drew a square, and drew a line down the middle.

"What would this part be called?" asked Lynne, pointing to one of the halves.

"Somebody else's part," replied Hugh.

"It's a rectangle," Irene added.

Aaron jumped in, "It's one half."

Hugh returned to his seat.

"Any other ideas?" Lynne asked.

Demetrius said, "Division is the math word for dividing."

Justine volunteered next. "Numbers divided by other numbers, like 12 divided by 2 is 6, or 5 divided by 2 equals 2.5," she said.

"How did you get those answers?" asked Lynne.

"On the calculator," Justine answered. She is fascinated by calculators and uses them whenever she can.

"You can divide numbers," offered Matthew, "and you can divide pie, pizza, apples, and other things."

Irene volunteered a specific example, "You could divide cookies if a friend came over. If there were four cookies, each person could have two."

Then Lynne asked, "What if I had nine cubes, and I wanted to divide them with Reggie? Could I divide them evenly?"

"Nooo," the class agreed.

"What is something else that you can't cut up to share equally?" continued Lynne.

Answers came quickly: "Chicken—it's too messy." "An ice cream cone." "Rocks." "A board eraser." "A book."

"What are some things that *can* be divided equally, even if there is a leftover piece?"

Students volunteered: "Pizza." "Cupcakes." "A sandwich."

Lynne then asked the children to return to their tables, talk together about what they knew about division, and write down their ideas. "Work together at your tables, and as a group write down as many things as you can that explain what you think division means and what kinds of things you think can be divided," she said. She circulated as the children discussed and wrote.

Table 2 wrote about separating things: *Taking one large number and seperating it into smaller nummbers.* Their paper showed how 32 could be divided into 16 2s.

The children at Table 2 included a numerical example in their paper.

Table 2 Division

1. Seperating things into groups.

2 I think of seeing how much people get evenly.

3. Taking one large number, and seperating it into smaller nummbers.
32   2212122222 2 22222   16 2's

4. cutting things in half.

Brittany called Lynne over. "Irene says that division is like the opposite of times," she said.

Irene explained, "It's like when 5 times 5 is 25, to get the answer divided by 5, you go backwards."

"That's interesting," answered Lynne. "Can you write down that idea on your paper?"

Brittany wrote: *We think dividing is something to do with times. Like if you get 25 from 5 × 5 it = 25. So if you divide 25 it is 5 becos use it is like the oppisopice* [opposite] *of times table.*

Shannon recorded a similar idea for her group. She wrote: *Division is the oppsite of multiplication.* She also included on their paper: *Division is when you divide something to share.* Their paper showed a birthday cake ready to be cut.

Shannon's writing for her group related division to sharing pizza and a birthday cake.

Division
1. Division is the oppsite of multi-plication
2. To divide means to seperate.
3. Reminds me of pizza cut in pieces.
4. Division is when you divide something to share.

You have to cut a cake into pieces

The students at Table 5 began by drawing on Justine's previous observation: *Numbers divided by other numbers. Dividing is like 5 ÷ 2 = 2.5.*

Table 3 included thoughts about equal groups. They wrote: *We think of dividing things up evenly when you say dividing. When someone says division we think of pizza. How to cut it up so that each piece is fair. Truc thinks division is like splitting a candy bar*

After all the tables had written at least three statements on their papers, Lynne interrupted the students so they could share what they had written. "I'd like each group to choose someone to read just one thing from your paper," she instructed.

Wesley read for his table. "I didn't write this, but I'm going to read it," he began, and then read: *"Sometimes divison is in equal groups. Sometimes divison is not in equal groups. If there is three people then you can share 9 ballons but it won't work for four people."*

"It won't work if you wanted equal shares?" prompted Lynne.

"Yeah," Wesley nodded.

Wesley's group wrote about division and equal groups.

Table 3

1. I think divison is separating things into groups like people on a team.
2. Sometimes divison is in equal groups.
3. Sometimes divison is not in equal groups. If there is three people then you can share 9 ballons but it won't work for four people.

Aaron read next: *"To divide is to cut into pieces or put into groups. 10 pencils put in half is 5 on 1 side and 5 on the other."*

Cynthia read from Table 9's paper: *"Division is about seperating."*

Table 9's paper showed a range of ideas about division.

Division   tab69
1 Division is usually represented by pie.
2 Division is about seperating.
3 Division is about sharing
4 Division is For Subtrating Faster
5 I would expect to see this sign. ÷ I think the line is seperating the 2 dots.

Pie

Patricia read, *"Vivian thinks of giving every body a equal amount of cake."*

Demetrius was in the group with Patricia, but he was interested in reading something else from his group's paper. The others at his group had disagreed with his idea at first, and he was anxious to share it. He read, *"It's a line and two dots, you start at 13 pencils and they give to 3 people, but it wasn't enough. It wasn't equal."*

"So what do you do?" asked Lynne.

"Give one away," he said. "It would've been easier with 12."

After each group had reported, Lynne gave another direction. "How about one person from each table coming to the board and drawing something that shows us what your paper says?" she said. "Take a moment and decide who will come up and what he or she will draw."

Keith came up and drew a pizza divided into eight sections. It was hard to tell from his drawing if he understood the concept of equal portions, but he explained, "They're supposed to be the same amount. It's hard to draw."

Samantha drew eight dots to represent eight M&M's and circled two groups of four.

"Could you divide those M&M's into five groups, or three groups?" asked Lynne.

"Yes," replied several students.

"But they wouldn't be equal," said Gabrielle.

Courtney came to the board and drew a circle. "If you have four people, you can divide a pie like this," she said, dividing the circle into four quarters. "If you have two people, you can still divide the pie evenly." She erased one of the lines on the pie, leaving it divided into two equal portions.

"So you can divide a pie evenly into different numbers of pieces," Lynne commented.

Courtney continued to say that division is also "how many times a number goes into another." She gave an example: "If you have 36 apples, how many 6s go into 36. The answer is how many apples six people can eat."

Note: Lynne doesn't always have children write when she presents this assessment to introduce the unit. In some years, she relies only on the discussion to give her a sense of the children's prior experience. She acknowledges that writing typically gives her information about those children who didn't volunteer their thoughts and often clarifies the responses given during the class discussion. But, with an eye on the amount of assessment information she will get from children's writing throughout the unit, and on what the discussion reveals, Lynne at times opts against adding the writing component to the assessment. Decisions such as this one are at the heart of the art and craft of teaching.

CONTENTS

Sharing Money   22
The Doorbell Rang   32
Dividing Cookies   49
The Game of Leftovers   60
Explorations with Raisins   72

WHOLE CLASS LESSONS

Five whole class lessons are suggested for this unit. Each approaches division from a different perspective.

In the first lesson, *Sharing Money,* students encounter division in a real-world context as they work in groups of four to investigate how to divide $5.00 and then 50 cents evenly among four people.

The children's book *The Doorbell Rang* provides the context for the second whole class lesson. In the story, two children are ready to share 12 cookies when additional friends and family begin to arrive to share the cookies. The lesson presents children with a series of division problems.

The third lesson, *Dividing Cookies,* requires a geometric interpretation of dividing, as the students divide paper circles (the "cookies"). Children report how much each child gets, revealing what they know about fractional symbols.

The Game of Leftovers is the fourth whole class lesson. This game gives children concrete experience with division problems with remainders.

In the fifth whole class lesson, *Explorations with Raisins,* students estimate the number of raisins in a box and gain experience with statistical reasoning and division.

Three of the lessons lead to independent activities on the menu. "A Suggested Daily Schedule" on pages 9–11 suggests a possible day-by-day plan that indicates how to intersperse whole class lessons with menu activities.

WHOLE CLASS LESSON   Sharing Money

Overview

This activity gives children a real-world problem-solving experience with division as they share $5.00, and then 50 cents, among four people. Most children this age have had enough experience with money to be able to handle small amounts abstractly. They know there are four quarters in one dollar and can proceed from that knowledge without having money in front of them. (As with all mathematical concepts, however, some children will find it helpful to have a concrete reference, and you may want to make play money available.)

Before the lesson

Gather these materials:
■ Play money, if needed

Teaching directions

■ Tell the students a story about four children who find a five-dollar bill. They give it to the principal who explains that she will keep it for a week in case anyone claims it. If no one has done so after a week, the children can have the money. When the children return to the principal in a week, she tells them that they can have the $5.00 with one condition: They must divide it equally among themselves.

■ Explain to the students that their task is to work in groups of four and determine how they would divide $5.00 equally among themselves. (If some groups have only three students, have them pretend to have four in their group.)

■ When students have solved this problem, ask them to figure out how to divide 50 cents among four people.

FROM THE CLASSROOM

Lynne began the lesson by gathering the class at the front of the room and telling the following story: "Four children were walking to school together and found a five-dollar bill. They brought it to the principal, and she told them, 'I'll keep it for a week to see if anyone comes to claim it. At the end of the week, if no one has claimed it, it's yours.'

"At the end of the week, no one had claimed the five-dollar bill, and so the principal told the children they could have it. 'But you have to do one thing,' she said. 'You must share the five dollars equally among the four of you.'"

Then Lynne explained the activity. "When you get into your groups," she said, "you need to discuss how you would share $5.00. Since you are going to collaborate on your answer, your group needs only one paper. Your explanation should use words, numbers, and, if you like, pictures to describe what each of you would get and how you solved the problem."

Anticipating that groups would finish the problem at different times, Lynne added, "As soon as you're finished, your whole group should come and talk to me. The whole group must come," she emphasized. "I'll talk with you and then give you another problem." The second problem was to find out how four children could share 50 cents equally. Lynne knew that this problem would be more difficult for the children because

the solution wasn't as visual and, when 50 cents was divided, money would be left over.

Observing the Children

The children were excited about the story and eager to share stories about times when they had found money. At his table Aaron told the group, "That once happened to me, but there was only one kid with me, and it was $1.00." The group talked for a few minutes about money children had found. Then Aaron suggested, "Everybody should draw a kid with the $5.00." Aaron went first. By the time most groups had solved the problem, Aaron was still drawing an intricate head. Lynne suggested that the other members of the group draw at the same time. Keith, Ethan, and Hugh liked this idea. The boys produced a visual representation of how the five-dollar bill was split four ways.

Aaron, Keith, Ethan, and Hugh spent a good deal of time on their drawings and showed their solution visually.

At his table Matthew immediately announced, "Well it's $1.25." No one paid any attention, but the other students in the group quickly came up with the same answer—also in their heads—and Matthew volunteered to write up their explanation. He concentrated on drawing a realistic dollar bill. "That's George Washington," he explained. "If I'd drawn the five-dollar bill, I would've drawn Abraham Lincoln."

Matthew recorded for his group, referring in his explanation to their school principal, Mrs. Rosen.

When Matthew, Irene, Brenna, and Ashley showed their answer to Lynne, she suggested that they try sharing 50 cents among the four of them. "That should be easy," Irene said. "It's smaller."

"I think we get 15 cents each," Matthew said.

Ashley wrote: *Each person gets $.15 if there are four people.* The others told her what else to write: *We think this because 15 + 15 + 15 + 15 equals 50. So you exchange the 50¢ piece for, four 10¢ and for, four 5¢ pieces.* However, before she was finished, the others realized that the answer wasn't correct.

"It's too much," Irene said. "That's 60 cents."

"Uh, oh," Brenna added. "What do we do?"

As Irene, Brenna, and Matthew talked, Ashley kept writing. She added: *Opssie* [Ooopsie] *wrong one Whoops thats 60¢.* Brenna found some play money, and the group figured out the answer. Ashley finally wrote: *Each person gets 12¢. In order to get twelve cents for each person you have to have 4, 10¢ pieces and 8 1¢ pieces.* They ignored the remainder.

Truc, Kyle, and Tano were a group of three, and they decided to change the problem to dividing $5.00 evenly among three people. First Truc tried adding $1.25 + $1.25 + $1.25 and got $3.75. The boys talked over that answer. "We need a lot more," they agreed. So Truc tried adding $1.50 three times and got $4.50. "More!" urged Tano. Truc added $1.80 three times, made a calculation error, and wrote the answer as $4.40, still not right. Using $1.90 gave them $5.70, so they tried $1.70. Still too high. Next came $1.60, then $1.65. With $1.66 + $1.66 + $1.66, they got a total of $4.98. So they tried $1.68. That total was $5.04, so they tried $1.67. That total of $5.01 was still too high, so they returned to $1.66 + $1.66 + $1.66, deciding that they could write *2 cents left over.*

They had completed all the addition using paper and pencil, but now Truc decided to check the results with the calculator. They were pleased to see that their total agreed with the calculator total and were proud to show their work to Lynne.

The boys then tackled the problem of sharing 50 cents. Totally immersed in the problem, this group remained working when the other children later gathered at the front of the room to discuss their results.

Matthew, Irene, Brenna, and Ashley made a false start before finally figuring out how to share 50 cents.

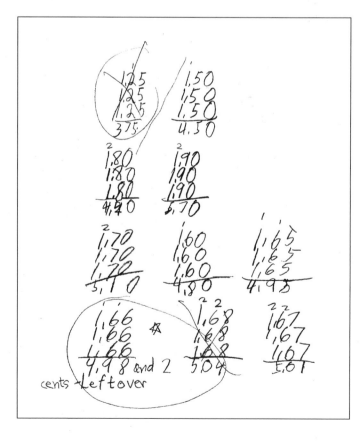

$ .50 ¢

Each person doesn't get $ .15 ¢ if there are four people.

We think this because $15 + 15 + 15 + 15 equals 50. So you exchange the 50¢ piece for, four 10¢ and for, four 5¢ pieces.
Oppsie wrong one
Whoops thats 60¢.

Each person gets 12¢. In order to get twelve cents, for each person you have to have 4, 10¢ pieces and 8 1¢ pieces.

Truc, Kyle, and Tano used trial and error to figure out how to share $5.00 among the three of them.

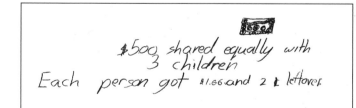

$500 shared equally with 3 children
Each person got $1.66 and 2 ¢ leftover.

As soon as Calie, Cynthia, Kent, and Garrett started working on sharing $5.00, Garrett said, "I'd go to the store and get all quarters. There are four quarters in one dollar."

"There are eight quarters in two dollars," offered Calie. Garrett glowered at her. He wrote an 8 on the paper, crossed it out, and turned his back on the group.

Calie and Cynthia started working together, and Kent and Garrett began to talk together about the problem. When she began writing, Calie wrote all four students' names on the paper when, in reality, only she and Cynthia were working together.

Calie explained how she and Cynthia shared $5.00 among four people.

Sharing A equally
$5.00

We exchanged the $5.00 dollar bill to a stor keeper for 5 $1.00 dollar bills & give @ person one dollar. We will have $1.00 left then we gave it to one of our mother & exchanged for four quarters each person got 1.25.

Meanwhile, Garrett decided that since he and Kent were now a group of two, the problem must change. "How would we share $5.00 between us equally?" he asked. Garrett decided to draw the problem. "Here's the principal," he told Kent. He drew several interactions between the principal and children. Garrett got frustrated when he couldn't come up with a mathematical solution to the problem and finally depicted the principal saying, "Go away."

Kent decided to draw as well, and his drawing showed that he had solved the original problem, giving $1.00 plus 25 cents to each of four people. Kent seemed to enjoy Garrett's company and did not mention that he had solved the problem.

Garrett and Kent then asked Lynne for another problem. She gave them the 50-cents problem, asking Garrett how he would share 50 cents with another person. She nudged a little, asking, "How many quarters are in 50 cents?" Garrett repeated the question, then started counting by 1s. He reached 33 and said, "Oops! I went too far." He tried adding several doubles—20 plus 20, 25 plus 25, and so on. Then he and Kent wrote the solution, Garrett writing the first sentence and Kent the second.

Garrett was not able to solve the problem.

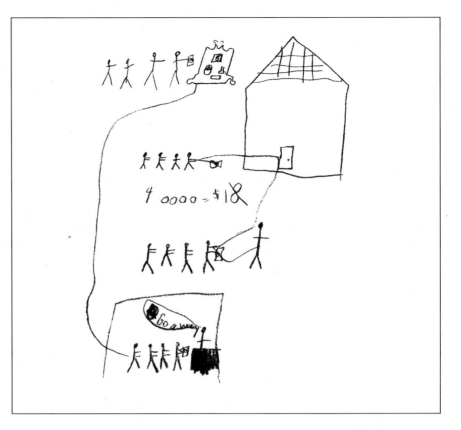

Kent showed his solution visually.

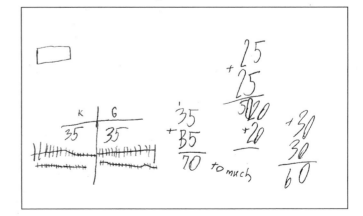

Garrett and Kent worked on splitting 50 cents between the two of them

Lynne wasn't sure whether Garrett didn't understand money or was just worried about writing answers. She knows he has serious learning problems and participates in a pullout program for special needs, but she feels positive about having him in her class. She resolved to explore his money sense with manipulatives—in this case real money—and to talk with his parents about giving him experiences with making change when they go to the store.

Calie and Cynthia began working on the sharing-50-cents problem, again pretending there were four people. This time, however, they didn't put all four names on their paper. They wrote: *Each person gets 12c. First we changed the 2 quarters into 5 dimes and we gave each person 1 dime. Then we exchanged the one dime into 10 pennies and gave each person 2 pennies and got 2 pennies left.*

When tackling the 50-cents problem, Reggie told his group. "This is easy. Get two circles and split them in half."

"You can't do that with money," protested Justine.

"Oh, right," groaned Reggie. "Let's get a calculator."

A Class Discussion

Near the end of the period Lynne gathered the children on the floor at the front of room and asked each group to report its findings. "If you solved more than one problem," she said, "choose one to report. Listen carefully to one another to see if you understand how each group got its answer."

Justine reported how she, Vivian, Reggie, and Wesley shared $5.00. "There are four kids and four dollars," she said. "Then we took a dollar away and got four quarters. So each kid gets one quarter and one dollar."

Justine, Vivian, Reggie, and Wesley clearly explained how to share $5.00.

> Table 6
>
> 5⁰⁰ Problem
>
> Each person will get 1.25. We know this because there are 4 quarters in a dollar and there are 4 kids. That takes 1 dollar away. There are 4 dollars and 4 kids. So each kid will get 1 quarter and 1 dollar.

Demetrius, Carey, Gabrielle, and Patricia also reported how they shared $5.00. They had drawn the five-dollar bill and then showed with pictures how they exchanged it for four dollar bills, two quarters, four dimes, and two nickels. *(Their work appears on the next page.)*

"You didn't have to use dimes and nickels," Matthew commented.

"But it worked," said Demetrius, defending their work.

Lynne commented to the class about the legitimacy of different methods of reporting mathematical investigations. "There's more than one way to solve the problem," she said. "Some groups explained with pictures and others with words. Some exchanged just for quarters and others for dimes and nickels as well."

Demetrius, Carey, Gabrielle, and Patricia pictured how they shared $5.00.

Brittany, Shannon, and Amari reported on an extra problem they solved: sharing $3.00 equally among four people. They found that each person would get 75 cents.

Brittany, Shannon, and Amari solved an additional problem of sharing $3.00 among four people.

Courtney, Jamie, Kent, and Veronica then reported their trial-and-error method for dividing 50 cents. They shared the reading of their paper: *"We tried 15 cents it was to much because it was 60¢. Then we tried 5 cents it was to little. Then we tried 7, 8, 9, 4, 10, 2, then we tried 11. Then we found that we would each get 12 because we looked it up on the calculator. They would have two remainders."* Although they didn't write it on their worksheet, Courtney reported that the group also tried 13. "Just to be sure," she said.

Courtney, Jamie, Kent, and Veronica used trial and error to reach a solution.

Sharing 50 ¢

We tried 15¢ it was to much because it was 60 ¢.

Then we tried 5¢ it was to little Then we tried 7, 8, 9, 4, 10, 2, then we tried 11

Then we found that we would each get 12 because we looked it up on the calculator. They would have two remainders.

Truc, Tano, and Kyle then joined the discussion. Lynne announced to the class, "Truc, Tano, and Kyle solved the problem of dividing $5.00 among three people. Just think: If you were in a group of three, how would you do it?"

Two able math students in the class quickly became engrossed in this new problem. Aaron said, "I'd give $1.00 to each person. That uses up three of the dollars." As he spoke, Lynne recorded his explanation numerically on the board:

$$\$3.00 = \$1.00 + \$1.00 + \$1.00$$

Then Aaron explained, "I'd change the two dollars left for quarters— that's eight quarters." Lynne wrote:

$$\$2.00 = .25 + .25 + .25 + .25 + .25 + .25 + .25 + .25$$

Aaron continued, "Each person would get two quarters; that leaves two quarters left over. I'd change those quarters to dimes and give everybody a dime. Now there's 20 cents left over . . . "

"Nickels!" shouted Demetrius, "Everybody gets a nickel and you have 5 cents left over. Five cents remainder."

"No, it's 2 cents remainder," Truc interrupted. "Can I write on the board?" Lynne nodded.

"Each person gets $1.66, and there are 2 cents left over," Truc explained, and wrote:

1.66
1.66
1.66
―――――
4.98 R2

Aaron and Demetrius applauded. "They got it down farther than we did!"

Lynne asked, "What's something you have to do when you're sharing money and things don't come out equally? What do you do with leftovers?"

Truc answered, "You can buy something you can all share."

"Throw it in the sea and make a wish," suggested Demetrius.

Irene, Matthew, Brenna, and Ashley explained how they broke 50 cents into its components, reporting, "We traded for 4 dimes and 10 pennies."

Ethan reported that he, Aaron, Keith, and Hugh had found 12 cents to be the answer for sharing 50 cents.

"How did you decide on 12?" asked Lynne.

"First we tried 14. Then we saw that was too much, so we tried 12," explained Ethan, describing a trial-and-error method similar to the one used by Courtney's group.

Having students explain their thinking strategies is valuable, not only for the students who report but also for those who listen. Lynne planned to give children opportunities to share their reasoning throughout the unit.

This group commented that 24 cents was easier to share than 25 cents.

WHOLE CLASS LESSON   The Doorbell Rang

Overview

Sharing items in real-world contexts helps students link division and fractions to the world around them. *The Doorbell Rang* by Pat Hutchins introduces the lesson and provides the context for teaching students to connect standard division notation with problem situations. After hearing the story, students retell it with division sentences and draw pictures to show their understanding of the notation. Also, each child invents a sharing problem and writes a one-event sequel to the story. The menu activity *The Doorbell Rings Again* (see page 89) extends this lesson by giving students the chance to write their own stories.

Before the lesson

Gather these materials:
■ *The Doorbell Rang* by Pat Hutchins (See Children's Books section, page 185.)
■ 12-by-18-inch drawing paper

Teaching directions

NOTE Having children grapple with mathematical concepts within the context of an engaging children's book shows them that mathematics is everywhere around us, not just in textbooks and worksheets.

■ Read aloud *The Doorbell Rang* by Pat Hutchins. In this book Ma has baked enough cookies for two children to share, each getting six cookies. But then two friends arrive and are invited to share the cookies. The doorbell rings twice more, and additional friends enter to share the cookies. When there are 12 cookies and 12 children, the doorbell rings again, and the children are relieved to see Grandma enter with a tray full of cookies.

Some students might already be familiar with this book. However, tell them that when they hear it this time they should think about the mathematics in the story.

■ After reading the story, introduce the symbolism for division. Then review the story, recording the following division sentences on the board to represent each part of the story:

1. $12 \div 2 = 6 \qquad 2\overline{)12}^{\,6}$

2. $12 \div 4 = 3 \qquad 4\overline{)12}^{\,3}$

3. $12 \div 6 = 2 \qquad 6\overline{)12}^{\,2}$

4. $12 \div 12 = 1 \qquad 12\overline{)12}^{\,1}$

■ Have the students figure out the number of cookies on the new tray that Grandma delivers.

■ Pose another problem. Say: "Suppose that Grandma had only 18 cookies on the new tray. How many cookies would there then be altogether?" After the children figure out that there would be 30 cookies, add another equation to the list on the board:

5. $30 \div 12 = \qquad 12\overline{)30}$

■ Explain to the students that they will retell the story with mathematical equations and illustrations, find the answer to 30 divided by 12, and finally invent an additional episode for the story, write a division sentence, and then solve it.

■ Show students how to fold a sheet of 12-by-18-inch paper into eight sections like this:

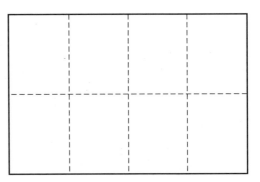

■ Explain that in the first box, students should write *The Doorbell Rang* and their own name. In the next four boxes, they retell the story, writing the mathematical equations numbered one through four that you listed on the board. In the sixth box, they write, solve, and illustrate the problem of dividing 30 by 12. In the remaining two boxes, the children make up a final part of the story. Add to the list on the board:

6. You finish the story.

■ After students have completed the assignment, hold a class discussion, asking students to share their stories and explain how they illustrated the mathematics.

FROM THE CLASSROOM

Lynne invited the children to sit on the floor at the front of the room to listen to a story. The children recognized an old friend in *The Doorbell Rang*.

"Yes," acknowledged Lynne, "I know it's a book that many of you read in first or second grade. What do you remember about it?"

"There were cookies," said Esme.

"More people kept coming," added Aaron.

"Were there more cookies?" Lynne asked.

"Noooo," said several students.

"So what did they have to do?"

"Divide them up!" several students replied in a chorus.

Lynne continued the introduction. "I'm going to read this book aloud, and I'd like you to think about the math in the story. I don't mean first-grade math, like counting the tiles on the kitchen floor. We're going to look at a different kind of mathematics."

Lynne stopped after reading the first page, when Ma tells her two children to share the cookies she made. "How many cookies did Sam and Victoria each get?" asked Lynne.

"They both had six," volunteered Tano.

"How could you say that mathematically?" Lynne asked.

"It's 6 plus 6 equals 12," Tano responded.

"Or," added Lynne, "if you wanted to use multiplication, you could say that two groups of 6 make 12." The children had recently completed a unit on multiplication.

Lynne continued reading the story, pausing to let the children figure out how many cookies each person gets as new guests arrive. Each time the doorbell rings announcing more people, Lynne asked the children to state a mathematical sentence for the cookie distribution. When they stated it as addition, she agreed and restated it as multiplication.

When she finished the story, Lynne asked, "Did the book ever say how many cookies there were?"

"No," chorused the children.

"No," agreed Lynne. "It said two children would get 6 cookies each, and you were able to figure out mathematically that Ma had given them 12 cookies. I'd like you to tell me what happened in the story, and I'll show you two ways to write it mathematically. So, what happened in the first part of the story?"

Keith raised his hand. "The mother made 12 cookies and divided them by 2. And 12 divided by 2 is 6," he said. Lynne wrote on the board:

$$1. \quad 12 \div 2 = 6$$

Lynne pointed to the division symbol and said, "This is the division sign and we read it as 'divided by.' The equation says '12 divided by 2 equals 6.'"

Lynne then showed another way to record. "You can also write '12 divided by 2 equals 6' like this." She wrote:

$$2 \overline{)12}^{\,6}$$

"What does the 12 stand for?" Lynne asked, pointing to the 12s in both of the mathematical recordings.

"Cookies," responded Ashley.

"What does the 2 mean?" Lynne pointed to the 2s.

"Two people," said Ethan.

"And the 6 is how many cookies each person got," Lynne concluded. "Okay, what was the next part of the story?" As students gave answers and talked about them, Lynne wrote the equations on the board. Finally, she had recorded:

1. $12 \div 2 = 6$ $2\overline{)12}^{\,6}$

2. $12 \div 4 = 3$ $4\overline{)12}^{\,3}$

3. $12 \div 6 = 2$ $6\overline{)12}^{\,2}$

4. $12 \div 12 = 1$ $12\overline{)12}^{\,1}$

"These tell mathematically what happened in the story," Lynne said, pointing to the board. "What happened the next time the doorbell rang?"

The children responded enthusiastically. "Grandma came!" "She baked more cookies." "She brought lots more."

"Let's figure out how many more cookies grandma brought," Lynne said. "She has them in rows." Lynne showed the class the page from the book, and the children counted along with her. When they found out that there were 12 rows with six cookies in each, Calie ran to get a calculator. But Matthew, proud of knowing his multiplication facts, called out the answer, "It's 72 cookies!" Lynne asked Calie to confirm Matthew's answer on the calculator.

"But 72 cookies makes a tough problem for the story. Let's change it and pretend that Grandma brought 18 more cookies. How many cookies would then be on the plate altogether? How much is 18 plus 12?" The children figured out that 30 cookies would be on the plate, and Lynne wrote on the board:

$$5. \quad 30 \div 12 = \quad 12\overline{)30}$$

Lynne then held up a sheet of 12-by-18-inch drawing paper. She said, "Each of you will get a sheet of paper like this and fold it into eight parts, like this." She folded the paper.

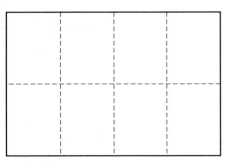

"On this paper, you'll retell the story, recording mathematically and drawing pictures to illustrate the division. In the first box of your paper, write the title of the story, *The Doorbell Rang*, and your name." Lynne pointed to the first box on her paper.

"In the next four boxes, write the four equations about the story as I did on the board." She pointed to equations 1 through 4 on the board. "For each equation, draw a picture to show how you would divide the cookies in the story." To illustrate what she meant, Lynne drew on the board a sketch of two children with six cookies each and wrote the mathematical sentence.

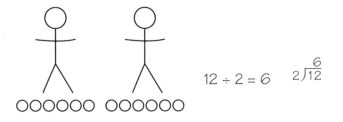

$$12 \div 2 = 6 \qquad 2\overline{)12}^{\,6}$$

"Do we write the numbers both ways?" Gabrielle asked.

Lynne thought for a moment. "That's up to you," she responded. "You can write it both ways or use just one, as long as you record some mathematical way to describe what happened." Gabrielle nodded.

"That leaves three more boxes on the paper," Lynne continued. "In the next one, write problem number 5 from the board, find the answer, and draw a picture to show how you would divide 30 cookies among 12 children. In the last two boxes, you finish the story. Pretend the doorbell rings again. Then you decide: Did more people arrive, or more cookies, or both? It's up to you." Lynne wrote one more item on the board:

6. You finish the story.

Lynne instructed each table to designate someone to get the sheets of drawing paper for his or her group. She added a reminder. "Be sure to show the story visually, along with the mathematical notation."

Observing the Children

Most of the students quickly folded their papers into eight parts. After 5 minutes, however, Matthew, who is proud of his mastery of multiplication facts, was unsure of what to do with the paper. Other students at his table finally explained how to fold it into eight parts. Matthew was baffled by the idea of picturing 12 divided by 2. He asked Lynne for help, and she talked with him, referring him to what she had drawn on the board.

Kyle concentrated on artistic lettering. He went immediately to the last box and began drafting "The End" in big block letters. After about 15 minutes, Lynne asked him to get started on picturing the mathematics.

As Lynne came near Brittany's desk, Brittany said, "I know! I'm just going to have 18 more people come to the door and then each gets one cookie." Then she changed her mind. "No, I'm going to have 8 more people."

"So there will be 20 people now," Lynne commented.

"Yeah, so each person gets one . . . one and a half cookies." Brittany wrote $30 \div 20 = 1.5$, displaying her understanding of the decimal notation for one-half.

Reggie, sitting next to Brittany, thought aloud, "12 divided by 4 is . . . 4? Am I right? 8? . . . Every answer is 8, right?"

"No," offered Demetrius sitting across the table from Reggie. "They're all different."

"I don't get it," complained Reggie. "What am I supposed to do? I don't get it." After a few minutes of insisting he didn't understand the problem, Reggie drew 12 cookies and wrote the equation in the first box. Then he drew 12 cookies again and wrote the second equation in the next box. He brought his paper to Lynne.

"This is a good beginning," she said, "but your drawings aren't complete. They show the 12 cookies but not how many people there were to share them."

"I don't know what to do," Reggie said.

"How many people were there in this box?" Lynne asked, pointing to the box in which Reggie had written $12 \div 4 = 3$.

"Four," he answered easily.

"I have a suggestion," Lynne said. She wrote in the 12 circles he drew: *1, 2, 3, 4, 1, 2, 3, 4, 1, 2, 3, 4.*

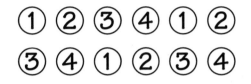

"This shows one way to divide the cookies among four people," she said.

"Oh, I get it," Reggie said, and returned to his seat. Reggie used this method while working independently on boxes three and four. He was struggling to represent 30 ÷ 12 when the recess bell rang.

Truc is a careful, methodical worker who hates to be interrupted in a math lesson before he has found an answer. He will always opt to forgo recess games to finish math, particularly if it means he will receive one-on-one attention from Lynne. He asked to stay inside during recess to finish his work. During this time, he came up with the answer to 30 ÷ 12: *2 each and 6 left over.* Lynne had not mentioned remainders.

"What are you going to do with the six leftover cookies?" asked Lynne

"Give them to Grandma and Mom." He wrote: *Mom eat 3. Grandma 3.*

The Next Day

When school began the next day, Reggie rushed into the classroom shouting the answer to 30 divided by 12: "I know it! I know it! It's $2\frac{1}{2}$!"

"How did you figure it out?" Lynne asked.

"Lucky guess." Reggie has difficulty communicating his mathematical understanding and frequently resorts to the "lucky guess" ploy.

To begin math time, Lynne asked the students to sit on the floor at the front of the room so she could review the work from the day before. "Let's look again mathematically at what happened in the story," she said. She wrote on the board to reinforce for the children the mathematical symbolization:

$$12 \div 2 \qquad 2\overline{)12}$$

"What does the 12 represent?" queried Lynne, not taking anything for granted and wanting to help students who were having difficulty keeping track of which number represented cookies and which represented children.

Lynne continued in this way to summarize the story, recording mathematically on the board:

$$12 \div 4 \qquad 4\overline{)12}$$

$$12 \div 6 \qquad 6\overline{)12}$$

Some children thought they saw a pattern of counting by 2s, offering 12 divided by 8 as the next equation.

Lynne suggested, "Let's look in the book." They quickly reviewed the story.

"After there were six children, then two more children came and brought their four cousins," Lynne said. "How many is that?"

"Six more," said Truc, "and 6 plus 6 equals 12."

Lynne confirmed Truc's answer and wrote on the board:

$$12 \div 12 \qquad 12\overline{)12}$$

"After you write these equations in the boxes, you will still have three boxes left," Lynne said. "Who remembers what goes in the next box?"

Irene raised her hand. "Next you do 30 divided by 12," she said.

"And you have to figure it out and draw a picture," Courtney added.

"But then you still have more room on your paper," Lynne said. "There are two more boxes, and you have to think about what might come next. What could happen if the doorbell rings again? What could you add?"

The children were quiet. Lynne suggested, "Maybe Father could come. He could bring more cookies. Or maybe he doesn't bring any cookies, but also wants to eat cookies. That would make 30 divided by 13 instead of 30 divided by 12. You'd have to figure out 30 cookies divided by 13 people."

Irene had another idea. "Grandma could eat cookies."

"Grandpa could come," said Ashley.

"More kids could come," Hugh offered.

"Cats could come," said Courtney, who brings her favorite animal into every project she works on.

"Yes," agreed Lynne. "You can change the number of cookies, the number of people or animals, or both to make a new addition to the story."

Before the children returned to their tables to continue working on the story, Lynne asked some of them to share their works-in-progress with the class. She told the children to listen to one another and think about the ideas they heard. She wanted them to see that there are different ways to solve a problem.

"Who would like to show us how you're representing the cookies and the children?" she asked.

Amari volunteered, showing how she drew the cookies on plates and used lines to divide them among the correct number of children.

Amari drew cookies on a plate and used lines to divide them.

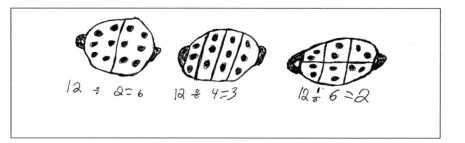

Lynne asked, "Who did it a different way?"

Keith showed how he put each person in a box and drew the cookies the person got to eat.

Keith drew faces of the children in separate boxes to show how many cookies they got.

12 Cookies
2 Children
12 ÷ 2 = 6

12 cookies
4 children
12 ÷ 4 = 3

Truc had drawn arrows, mapping people onto the number of cookies they received.

Truc used arrows to connect people to groups of cookies.

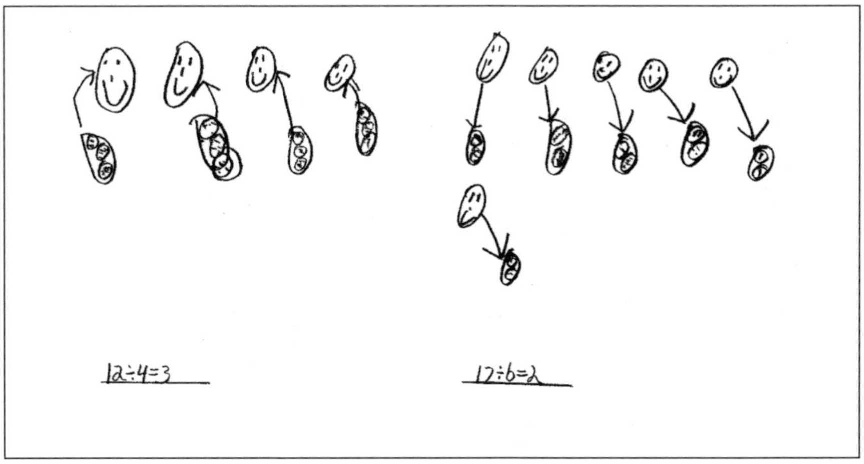

12 ÷ 4 = 3

12 ÷ 6 = 2

Lynne responded to the students' presentations by saying, "Notice the different ways people have done this. Remember, there's no one right way to do it. There are many ways to solve a problem." She then had the students return to work.

Soon after the children had started working, Irene indicated that she was finished. In each box, she had drawn the face of a person and the cookies underneath each person who received them. For 30 divided by 12, she showed $2\frac{1}{2}$ cookies for each child.

Irene illustrated how for 30 ÷ 12, each person would get 2¹/₂ cookies.

In his paper, Kent showed that he knew something about conventional notation, although sometimes he got it backward. This is typical for children as they are learning something new.

Kent used conventional division notation, but was confused as to where to put the numbers.

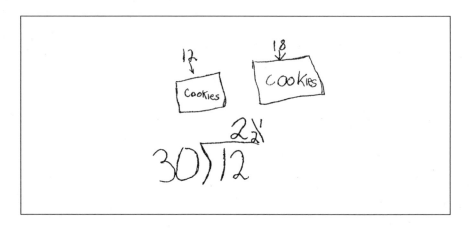

Children tried various ways to write the notation for 2¹/₂:

Courtney: $2 + 1\frac{1}{2}$

Brenna: *2 in a half*

Cynthia: $2\frac{2}{1}$

Demetrius used a calculator and wrote the equation *30 ÷ 12 = 2.5,* followed by *(2 and a half)* to indicate he knew what the equation meant.

Carey, Ashley, and Veronica used calculators to divide. Ashley wrote *2.5* without questioning what it meant. When Lynne asked her why she wrote that answer, she shrugged, "I looked at the calculator." Lynne reminded her that she was to do only what made sense to her. Lynne suggested to Ashley that she talk with Veronica about how to explain the calculator answer.

Brittany also used a calculator, but she didn't notice the decimal point and wrote *25*. Amari, sitting next to Brittany, also wrote *25*.

"I don't think that's possible," Lynne said to the girls. "If there were 30 cookies altogether, how could each person get 25?"

The girls looked at each other. "We used the calculator," Brittany said, in defense.

"It's fine to use the calculator," Lynne said, "but you have to be sure that the answer makes sense. Show me what you did on the calculator."

Amari punched in 30 ÷ 12 and showed the calculator to Lynne.

"See that little dot between the 2 and the 5?" Lynne asked the girls. They nodded. "It's called a decimal point, and it's very important," Lynne continued. "It means that the answer is 2 and then some; 2.5 is more than 2 but less than 3. The .5 means one-half."

"What do we do?" Brittany asked, confused.

"If you want to use the calculator, then you have to write down exactly what the answer is, with the decimal point," Lynne continued. "But if it doesn't make sense to you, then you need to find some other way to solve the problem. You might talk with Kent or Courtney. They did it without a calculator." She left the girls to decide what to do.

Cynthia also used the calculator, but explained the answer of 2.5 by adding: *There is 6 left and you can cut it in hafe* 1/2.

Students had different ideas for their own episodes. In describing his own problem for one more ring of the doorbell, Reggie wrote the equation 15 ÷ 3 = 5. However, during much writing, counting, erasing, and rewriting, he lost track of what the numbers represented—cookies or people. A parent volunteer offered to help, but Reggie was frustrated and just kept insisting, "I don't get it."

"Which numbers were people in that box?" asked the volunteer, pointing to box two.

"Mrs. Zolli thinks the 2," grumbled Reggie. "But I don't think so. I think they're cookies."

"Well, in this last one," prompted the volunteer, "where did you get the 15?"

"I wanted it," insisted Reggie.

"Maybe it will help to begin this like a story," prompted the volunteer. "The doorbell rang . . . "

Reggie grinned. He said, "And my uncle came. He came with some cookies . . . 15 cookies."

"Where did you get the 3?"

"I don't know."

"What is the 5?"

"The 5 is the answer."

"What does it mean?"

"It's the kids . . . five kids."

NOTE Partial understanding and confusion are a natural part of children's learning. Children need many experiences and opportunities to talk about their thinking in order to grasp an idea firmly and learn how to represent it mathematically. Errors are to be expected when students grapple with new ideas.

Garrett, a boy with serious learning disabilities, is in a pullout program for special needs. This means that he misses part of math class. "Of course I wish he were here all the time," admits Lynne. "But I have to ask: What's best for Garrett? I think it's best for him to get that one-on-one attention."

Garrett started out eagerly on the problem. The day before, he had been very involved in spelling out words. He laboriously had copied the title *The Doorbell Rang* from the board, letter by letter. He stared at the board, then wrote a letter, stared at the board again, then wrote another letter. Today he wrote, *Thar was 12 cookies,* but he drew 13 circles. Then he counted and erased one. Writing and counting are laborious for Garrett, and it took him one period and part of another to produce this much work.

Carey, who also misses math to participate in a pullout program, used a calculator to solve the problems. His illustrations showed that he understood what numbers represented people in the equations; he drew them sitting around a table in each box. His cookies, however, were hard to make out because he had used a marker with a thick point to draw them. Carey was pleased with his sequel—that Santa Claus came with 50 more cookies. He didn't write an equation for his sequel, but he drew the cookies and wrote the number that appeared when he punched the equation into the calculator: 1.66666. (He had erroneously punched in 20 ÷ 12.)

Carey's illustrations showed his understanding of what the numbers represent.

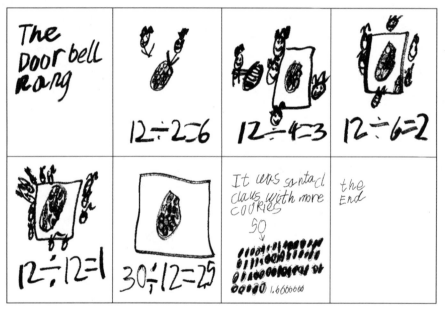

Carey didn't realize his error, or know what the string of 6s meant, but he was fascinated by them. He believed they would go on and on. "Sixes forever," he said, as he walked around the room with his paper, showing off the number. Lynne left Carey to his pleasure in that figure.

Demetrius liked the number, too. He wanted to try it. "What's the problem?" he asked Carey. Carey told him, "It's 50 divided by 12."

"I don't think that's possible," protested Demetrius. "With 50 cookies, they'd get more than 1 each." Using a different calculator from Carey's,

Demetrius punched in the numbers and got a different answer: 50 ÷ 12 = 4.1666667. "Lots of 6s, Carey, but not forever," concluded Demetrius.

When Kent tried a similar problem, he found a way to make sense of all the 6s he saw on the calculator. Noticing a tub of Unifix cubes next to him on the floor, Lynne asked Kent what problem he was trying to solve.

"I have to do 80 divided by 12," he answered.

"Are you going to use 80 cubes?" she asked.

"Yeah," he responded, "then I'm going to divide them out with my hands because the calculator doesn't make sense to me."

"What did the calculator say?" Lynne asked.

"It gave me a bunch of 6s," Kent answered. Lynne left him to continue working.

Aaron was using Unifix cubes to figure out 30 divided by 12. He counted out 30 cubes and then put them into eight piles of 3 each.

"I see that you have eight piles of 3s there," Lynne said. "Don't you want to divide the cookies for 12 people?"

He nodded and said, "So what do I do?"

"How many piles do you think you should have if you want to divide 30 cookies among 12 people?"

"Twelve?" he asked.

"Try that and see if it makes sense to you."

Aaron came to get Lynne when he had finished. He had 12 piles with 2 in each, and 6 extras.

"What are you going to do with the leftover cookies?" Lynne asked.

"I don't know," he responded

"Can you split a cookie in half?" she asked.

"Yes," he said.

"So if you cut the six leftovers in half, how many halves would you have?"

Aaron thought for a second and said, "Twelve. Oh, I know." He drew two boxes and a half circle next to each face on his paper. He recorded: $30 ÷ 12 = 2\frac{1}{2}$.

Juliette was involved with the idea of sharing 30 cookies. "Look," she told Lynne, "with two people, you get 15, and with three people you get 10."

"How did you figure that out?" Lynne asked.

"I just knew," Juliette responded.

"Could you figure out how to share 30 cookies among four people?" Lynne asked.

"Ooooh, I think so," Juliette said. Seizing on Juliette's interest, Lynne recorded on her paper:

2 people — 15
3 people — 10
4 people —

A few minutes later, Juliette came back to Lynne. "Mrs. Zolli, it doesn't come out even. There are two extras." Lynne showed her how to record the answer as *7 R2*. Juliette was pleased and, on her own, continued the list Lynne had started up to 12, figuring out how to share 30 cookies among each number of people.

Juliette figured out how to share 30 cookies among 2 through 12 people.

2 people — 15
3 people — 10
4 people — 7 R2
5 people — 6
6 people — 5
7 people — 4 R2
8 people — 3 R6
9 people — 3 R3
10 people — 3
11 people — 2 R8
12 people — 2 R6

NOTE There are two ways to think about division. Solving 12 ÷ 2, for example, can be accomplished by thinking about dividing 12 into groups of 2 each (resulting in six groups) or dividing 12 into two groups (with 6 in each). Either way produces the same answer, and either is appropriate when thinking about the numbers abstractly. When the problem is related to a context, however, although both approaches sometimes make sense, only one or the other actually relates to the action that the context dictates.

Ethan is recognized by his peers as a whiz with math facts. He also likes to draw detailed pictures to illustrate the complex stories he writes. While illustrating 30 divided by 12, he became so wrapped up in drawing people that he drew 18 people instead of 12. He didn't draw any cookies in the boxes. "Make sure you show the math in your picture," Lynne reminded him.

Ashley started out drawing two people and 12 cookies. Then she circled every 2 cookies. What she did made sense for solving 12 divided by 2 abstractly, but not in this context; instead of making groups of 2, Ashley needed to divide the cookies into two groups. Ashley is not a child who sits and struggles. When she jumped up and asked for help, Lynne helped her see how to divide the 12 cookies into two parts.

Ashley decided to name the people. She used the initials from the story but renamed them as Veronica and Shannon, two of her classmates. She drew too many people for 12 divided by 4, but after some struggle managed to get herself back on track, at the same time coming up with two more names.

After drawing 12 cookies and six people for 12 divided by 6, Ashley jumped up again for help. Lynne suggested that since Ashley had named the people, it might help if she labeled the 12 cookies with these names or their initials. Ashley liked this idea.

For 30 divided by 12, Ashley drew 30 cookies and left out the people altogether. The calculator gave her 2.5 for the answer but when Lynne asked her what the answer meant, Ashley didn't want to explain. "The calculator said so," she insisted. Ashley seemed exhausted by this problem, and Lynne decided not to push her at this time.

For her final box, Samantha decided that Grandpa comes home with 15 more cookies. She reported how she had used a calculator and got 45 ÷ 13 = 3.46. "What do I do?" she asked Lynne.

"How could you cut a cookie into that sort of weird number?" Lynne replied. Samantha shrugged. Lynne talked with her about leftovers. Samantha finished her story with *Give 6 cookies to the cat.*

In her last box, Samantha figured out how to solve 45 divided by 13.

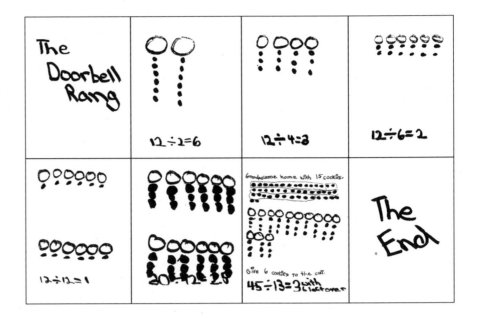

Truc seemed stuck on the last box. "Who will come and what will they bring?" prodded Lynne

"They bring 40 more cookies," grinned Truc.

"Okay, how many cookies will you have then?"

"There'll be 70 cookies and 15 people, counting Mom, Grandma, and the person who brought the 40 cookies," he answered.

"Can you write that?" asked Lynne

Truc nodded and went to work. This was a San Francisco classroom five days before the National Football League playoffs, and Truc wrote: *The Doorbell Rang it was Joe Montana and he brought 40 cookies but the children and Joe Montana and Grandma and Mom want more cookies.*

A Class Discussion

The next day, Lynne initiated a class discussion by inviting the students to present the events they had added to the story. Truc went first, explaining about Joe Montana bringing cookies. His solution to the problem was unconventional as he struggled to use fractions and remainders: *70 ÷ 15 = 4$\frac{1}{2}$ and 3 leftover.* He explained that the cat ate the extra three cookies. The others were impressed at how he had drawn and circled cookies to figure this out. (Truc's math was not exact—there should have been 2$\frac{1}{2}$ remaining, not 3. But he was struggling with a big concept, and for a first stab he did just fine.)

Another football fan, Demetrius, ended his story with Steve Young, the 49er quarterback, bringing 30 more cookies. Demetrius is mathematically savvy and was aware that by adding 30 cookies and no people (he didn't include the quarterback in the total), he was writing a sharing problem that would be easy for him to solve.

Kyle used the idea of leftovers: *30 ÷ 12 = 2 each and 6 leftover.* Then he found people to eat the leftovers: *Mom 3 and Grandma 3.* In the last box, when the doorbell rang again, *It was Arnold Schwarsanager. He brought 50* more cookies. *80 ÷ 15 = 5 each with 5 left over.* Kyle decided the leftovers should be given to Arnold. "Nobody argues with Arnold," he insisted.

In his sequel, Wesley had 3 more people arrive so the 30 cookies were shared among 15 people. He wrote: *The doorbell rang Joe and his 2 cousins came to eat some cookies. 30 ÷ 15 = 2.*

Wesley's illustration of half cookies for 30 ÷ 12 showed that he understood the meaning of 2.5.

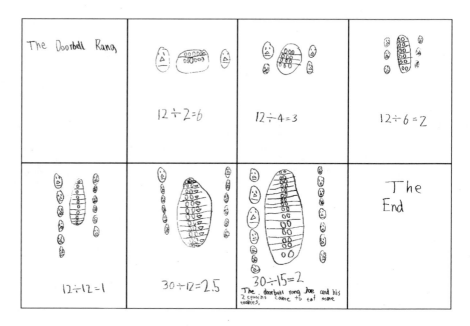

For his sequel, Aaron wrote: *Then grandpa came in with a giant cookie. And he splits the cookie into 12 pieces. So each kid got 2½ cookies and a triangle.* "He cut it like a pizza," he explained.

Aaron solved 12 ÷ 4, then added a sequel with a giant cookie.

Jamie is fond of bunnies and often includes them in her work. Here, a bunny gets the 6 extra cookies left over from sharing 44 among 12 children.

For his sequel, Ethan had four people arrive to share the 30 cookies—one mom, one grandma, and two extras.

Amari had decided that in the final frame, when the doorbell rang, one person was there, wanting cookies. She had been stumped at first by the problem of 30 divided by 13, and she explained to the class what she had done. "I took counters and made double-decker," she said. "But then there were two extras. So I made three-decker cookies. That didn't work. Then Mrs. Zolli told me I could have leftovers, so I did double-deckers with four cookies left over."

Lynne then raised the issue of using calculators. "I noticed when some of you used the calculator, you got strange numbers," she said. "For example, when you divide 30 by 14, you get 2.1428571." She wrote that num-

ber on the board. "Now that is a very strange number," she continued. "We don't talk about cookies with this number. So for this problem, the calculator answer doesn't make sense. But when you do 30 divided by 12, you get 2.5." She wrote that on the board.

"Some of you remembered from before that .5 equals one-half, so you can make sense of the calculator answer," she said. "But I'd solve 30 cookies divided among 14 people a different way. I'd figure it out by myself. Do you think everyone will get 1 cookie?" Lynne quickly drew 30 circles on the board. The children nodded.

"Can everyone get 2 cookies?" she then asked. The students figured out that if everyone got 2 cookies, there would be 2 left over. Lynne showed them how to record this mathematically:

$$30 \div 14 = 2 \text{ R2} \qquad 14\overline{)30}^{\,2\,\text{R2}}$$

Lynne continued, "Let's do 30 divided by 12 this way. Talk to your neighbor about how many cookies each person would get and how many would be left over."

After a few minutes, Lynne asked what they had found out. Gabrielle reported that everyone got 2 cookies, with 6 extras. Lynne wrote on the board:

$$30 \div 12 = 2 \text{ R6} \qquad 12\overline{)30}^{\,2\,\text{R6}}$$

A number of students insisted that the answer was $2\frac{1}{2}$; they were anxious to show that they had the "right" answer and didn't want to hear about the remainder.

Lynne had the last word: "You can write remainders two ways, as leftovers or as fractions."

Lynne tabulated some results of this introductory lesson:

Children using conventional notation for division: All

Children relying on calculator answers (2.5) without understanding: 7

Children relying on calculator answers (2.5) with understanding: 4

Children cutting cookies in many parts so there is no remainder: 1

Children using remainders: 7

Children whose work was still incomplete: 9

Children planning last box to make mathematics easy: 3

Children writing fractions conventionally: 4

Children writing fractions with some but not complete accuracy: 8

Lynne knew that the children would have many more opportunities to think about division, with and without remainders, so she chose to move on to the next lesson in the unit. The children who hadn't finished would have time to do so when menu time began.

WHOLE CLASS LESSON Dividing Cookies

Overview

Dividing Cookies gives children division experience that engages them with fractions and provides the geometric challenge of dividing circles into equal parts. In contrast to the first two whole class lessons, this lesson requires using more than counting to solve problems; children must think spatially as they divide various numbers of circles ("cookies") into four equal shares. Asking children to report how much each child gets reveals what they know about the symbolism of fractions.

Before the lesson

Gather these materials:
■ Cookies worksheet, duplicated on colored paper, at least two per group (See Blackline Masters section, page 196.)
■ Dividing Cookies recording sheet, five per group (See Blackline Masters section, page 195.)
■ Scissors
■ Glue

Teaching directions

■ Cut out a few paper cookies.

■ Tell the children that they will be sharing paper cookies. Show them the ones you cut out and the duplicated worksheets of cookie patterns. Explain that they will have to cut out the cookies they'll use.

■ To help students think about dividing cookies into equal shares, ask: "Suppose a group of four had four cookies. How much would each person get if they shared the cookies equally?" The answer will be obvious to the children, but this is a good opportunity to discuss the concept of "sharing equally."

■ Explain that they will work in groups of four and solve several problems, first sharing six cookies, then five, three, two, and one cookie.

■ Show students the *Dividing Cookies* recording sheet and explain that they should first write each student's name at the top and fill in the number of cookies they are sharing. Then they take the number of paper cookies they need, divide them up, and paste each person's share in one box on the worksheet. Finally, they answer the question at the bottom of the worksheet: "How much did each person get?"

■ Explain that after solving the first problem of sharing six cookies, the group should check with you before continuing. Once you've checked the group's first solution, the group can continue with the other problems of sharing five cookies, three cookies, two cookies, and one cookie. Remind students that they should use a new recording sheet for each new problem.

■ Organize the class into groups of four students. If there are any groups with two or three students, tell them they should solve the problems as if there were four children, so they'll be able to compare their solutions with the others in the class.

■ After the students have solved all the problems, initiate a class discussion. Have students share their solutions for several problems. If you think it's needed or appropriate, take this opportunity to do some instruction about standard fractional notation.

FROM THE CLASSROOM

"Okay, class," Lynne began the lesson, "the good news is that today we are going to share cookies. The bad news is that these are the cookies." Lynne held up several 2-inch paper circles, and the children groaned.

She then held up a sheet of green copier paper covered with 2-inch-diameter circles. "We're going to cut out a lot of these circles and use them to figure out answers to some problems," she said. (The color of the paper doesn't matter; what matters is the contrast, so that when children cut and paste their cookies onto white paper, the fractional parts will stand out.)

Lynne then drew a circle on the board, divided it into fourths, and shaded three quarters of it. She asked, "Who can tell me how much of the circle is shaded?"

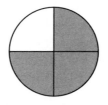

About a half dozen children raised their hands, and Lynne called on Aaron. "It's three-fourths," he said.

"That's right," Lynne confirmed. "I divided the circle into four parts and each part is called 'one-fourth.' Then I shaded in three of the four parts, so the part I shaded is called 'three-fourths.' It's also okay to say 'three-quarters.'"

The children remained quiet, so Lynne wasn't able to tell who understood, but she continued. "Does anyone know how to write 'three-fourths' or 'three-quarters'?" she asked.

Lara came to the board and wrote:

$$\frac{4}{3}$$

"You've used the right two numbers," Lynne said, "but you need to switch them. When there are three out of four parts, three-fourths, the first number goes on top and the second number on the bottom."

Lara rewrote the fraction correctly:

$$\frac{3}{4}$$

"We always say the top number first. It's 3 out of 4," explained Lynne, "so three-fourths of the circle is shaded."

Next Lynne drew a half circle on the board.

"How much is this?" she asked the class. About half of the students raised their hands.

"It's half," Wesley answered.

"Yes, it is," Lynne confirmed. "Can anyone tell how to write the number for 'one-half'?"

Courtney knew, and came to the board and confidently wrote:

$$\frac{1}{2}$$

Some of the other children nodded their agreement; many just watched. Lynne drew the rest of the circle using a dotted line.

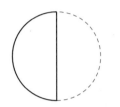

She explained, "What I drew to start with is one of two equal size pieces, so each is one-half. You write that with a 1 over a 2, just as Courtney did." Next, Lynne drew a circle and a half circle.

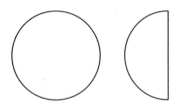

"This is one whole circle and one-half of a circle," she said, writing on the board as she spoke:

$$1 + \frac{1}{2}$$

"I can also write this another way, without the plus sign." She wrote:

$$1\frac{1}{2}$$

"I write the whole number big," she pointed out, "and the numbers in the fraction smaller."

Lynne wasn't sure what the children knew about fractions or the conventions of fractional notation, as she hadn't done any formal instruction with fractions as yet this year. Although she knew this brief introduction wouldn't be of much use to children who had no experience with the symbolism of fractions, she hoped that it would serve as a help or reminder to children who did have some prior experience.

Lynne then returned to explaining the cookie-sharing activity. "In this activity, you're going to share cookies in groups of four," she began. "Suppose your group has four cookies to share, how many will each person get if you make sure to share equally?" Lynne emphasized "share equally," an important concept when considering fractional parts.

NOTE At times, the common use of a term differs from the mathematical use of the same term. Although it's common to hear children say, "Your half is bigger than my half," it's important for them to understand that the same fractional parts of a whole must be the same size.

"One," children chorused.

Lynne acknowledged, "Okay, that was easy. You know about sharing." She then continued with the directions. "You're going to do this activity several times," she said, "each time starting with a different number of cookies. And each time, you'll show on a recording sheet the equal shares you make."

Lynne showed the students a sample recording sheet. (See Blackline Masters section, page 195.) "You'll use a new recording sheet each time you share a different number of cookies," she explained. "Each time you share the cookies equally among the four of you, cut them out of the green paper and paste each person's share in a box. Then, at the bottom of the recording sheet, describe what you did by answering the question, 'How much did each person get?'"

Lynne then wrote instructions on the board. "Your group will do five problems, sharing cookies five times," she explained as she wrote:

COOKIES	PEOPLE
6	4
5	4
3	4
2	4
1	4

"First your group will share six cookies, paste the shares on a sheet, and record how much each person got," Lynne said. "After you share six cookies equally, show me your paper, so I can check that you did it correctly. Then you'll get another recording sheet and do the same for five cookies. You'll share five times, using a different number of cookies each time."

Lynne then talked with the class about how the groups should work. "Decide in your group who will do the tasks that need to be done," she said. "One person will get the recording sheet; another person will get two sheets of cookies; one person will get four scissors; another person will have a pencil ready to write everyone's name on the recording sheet. For each different worksheet, someone else in your group should do the writing.

"Together, cut out the cookies you'll need. You might want to cut out just the six cookies for the first problem, or figure out how many you'll need for all five problems and cut them all out."

Lynne reminded the children what to do when their group finished sharing six cookies and recording the results. "Raise your hands, so I can come and check. Remember, every member of your group should be able to explain your thinking."

Observing the Children

Most children started work eagerly. Some groups cut out just the six circles they needed for the first problem; others cut out all of the circles.

Lynne noticed that Aaron, quick with numbers, added the numbers she had written in the Cookies column on the board. "We need 17," he said. Then he quickly counted to find there were 9 circles on a sheet. "Hey, we don't need to cut two whole sheets," he announced to his group.

When a group had difficulty, Lynne gave the students time to work out their problems. Today, for example, Matthew, Irene, Ashley, and Brenna

got off to a rough start. Ashley insisted on cutting out all of the cookies herself; Brenna fiddled with the ones she had already cut out; Matthew and Irene argued over who would write names on the recording sheet. The group finally settled down and quickly solved the first problem, had Lynne check it, and continued.

Other groups began work immediately, but not always as a team. Garrett protested as Calie, without consulting anyone else in the group, immediately started cutting all the cookies in half. Cynthia and Kyle didn't say anything, but Garrett insisted that Calie talk things over before cutting. Finally, Calie got up and went to another group, asking Truc, "Are you supposed to cut the cookies in half?"

Truc answered, "If you want to."

Calie returned to her group. By then, Cynthia had given everybody in the group one-half of a cookie. "It works," she said.

"See?" Calie said to Garrett, who remained silent.

This group understood the idea of equal sharing: When they shared three cookies, they labeled each person's share as *a half and a $\frac{1}{4}$*. For five cookies, they wrote *a whole cookies & $\frac{1}{4}$*.

When it was Garrett's turn to write, however, he said he didn't have a pencil. Garrett is frequently without a pencil, and it is class policy that when a child tells Mrs. Zolli that he or she doesn't have a pencil, she addresses the whole class: "Garrett needs a pencil. Does anyone have an extra he can borrow?" Today Garrett didn't tell Lynne that he needed a pencil. He told the members of his group, and they refused to lend him one. Prepared for this circumstance, Garrett grinned and reached into his desk, pulling out a pencil that was just a point of lead stuck into an eraser. The group was impressed, and Garrett was pleased by the attention they gave his labors to actually write with this smidgen.

When Matthew, Irene, Ashley, and Brenna got to the fourth problem, sharing two cookies among four people, they were unsure about how to write each person's share. They had written $1\frac{1}{2}$ and called to Lynne for help.

"Read your answer to me," Lynne said to them.

"One-half," Ashley and Matthew said in unison.

Having them read gave Lynne valuable information that they were able to construct equal shares and knew how much each person would get, but they weren't sure about standard fractional notation. Lynne explained to them that what they had written indicated that each person got a whole cookie and a half.

"Oh, I see," Irene said. "I can fix it."

"Make sure that everyone agrees," Lynne reminded her, and left the group to continue.

Truc, Tano, Kyle, and Brittany quickly solved the six-cookie problem. When they began to share five cookies, they discovered that they could create a new whole cookie if they grouped each person's fraction in the center of the page.

Brittany set herself the task of cutting all the cookies into quarters. She cut, and her partners figured out what kind of interesting arrangements they could make. These children concentrated on the design of the entire field of four rectangles. They wanted their answers to be right, but they also wanted them to look nice.

Truc, Tano, Kyle, and Brittany shared five cookies and showed how each person got 1¼ cookies.

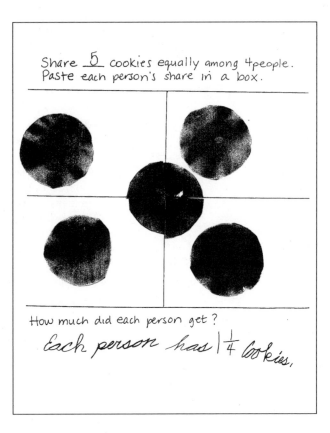

Truc, Tano, Kyle, and Brittany arranged the cookie shares in a pattern that pleased them.

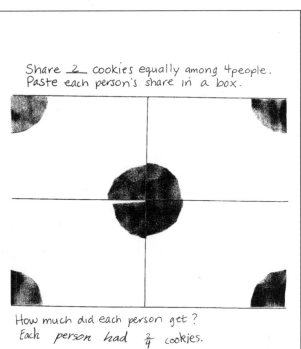

After solving the five required problems, Courtney, Jared, Kent, and Jamie decided to do an extra one, and shared seven cookies among four people.

Courtney, Jared, Kent, and Jamie solved an extra problem, sharing seven cookies.

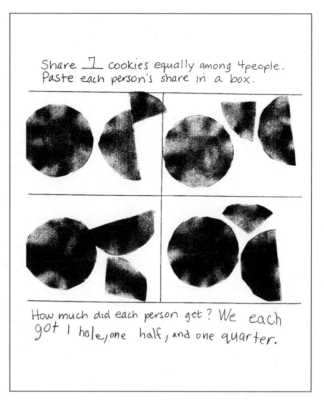

Share _7_ cookies equally among 4 people. Paste each person's share in a box.

How much did each person get? We each got 1 hole, one half, and one quarter.

A Class Discussion

Lynne called the children to the front of the room. "It's interesting to see how people represented their thinking," she said. "When you had one cookie and you had to share it with four people, how much did each person get?"

"One-fourth," Calie answered, holding up half of a cookie.

Rather than telling Calie she was wrong, Lynne asked her to explain her thinking. Calie said, "When you cut up a cookie into four parts, each part is one fourth." She looked at her piece. "Oh, this is a half," she corrected herself.

"Why do you think it's a half?" asked Lynne.

"Because two of these make one whole cookie," Calie answered.

Lynne wrote $\frac{1}{2}$ on the board, explaining, "This means 'one out of two,' and for four people Calie needs 'one out of four.'" She wrote $\frac{1}{4}$ on the board.

"Suppose I take another cookie," Lynne said. "If I talk about this cookie and one-fourth of a cookie, how much do I have altogether?"

Children chorused, "One and one-fourth."

"On your papers, when you shared five cookies," Lynne continued, "some of you wrote one and a fourth in words for each person's share. How would you write it in numbers?" She called on Demetrius, who walked up to the board and wrote:

$$1\frac{1}{4}$$

"What happened when you had to share three cookies?" Lynne then asked. She called on Matthew.

"We divided them in half and gave them out," he said. "But then we had two pieces left, so we divided them into quarters."

"How much did each person get?" Lynne asked.

"A half and a quarter," volunteered Amari. She showed the group's paper.

Justine, Wesley, Amari, and Reggie shared three cookies by giving each person a half and a quarter.

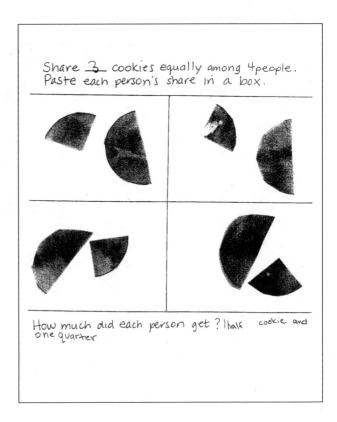

"Can I show how to write it in numbers?" Ashley asked. Lynne nodded. Ashley came up and wrote on the board:

$$\frac{1}{2} + \frac{1}{4}$$

"Did anyone divide three cookies a different way?" asked Lynne.

Keith was eager to show how his group had divided the cookies. "Each person got three quarters," he said, showing their paper. (*Keith's group's work appears on the next page*).

Do you know how to write 'three quarters' in numbers?" Lynne asked Keith. He shook his head. Truc volunteered, however, came to the board, and wrote:

$$\frac{3}{4}$$

Lynne commented about the solutions Amari and Keith showed. "Their answers are different," she commented. "Did each group divide the cookies equally among four people?"

Keith, Aaron, Ethan, and Hugh divided three cookies into quarters to share them.

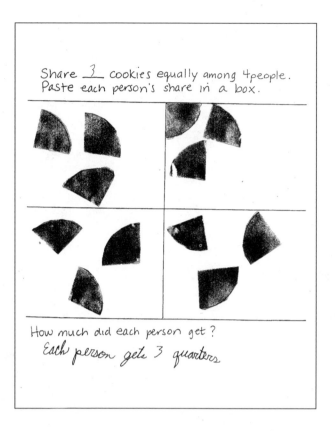

Share __3__ cookies equally among 4 people. Paste each person's share in a box.

How much did each person get?

Each person gets 3 quarters

Children disagreed. "No," insisted Reggie. "Keith's group got more cookies."

"Three-fourths means one-half plus one-fourth, so they're the same," said Aaron.

Other children joined in the discussion. Some agreed with Reggie that more pieces meant more cookies. Others could "see" that the half was made up of two quarters.

"Look," said Demetrius, going to the board and tracing a half cookie portion. Then he taped two one-fourth pieces on it.

"Wow!" Reggie was impressed.

Lynne explained, "Amari's group passed out halves, and then, when they needed to, they cut two halves in half, making quarters. Keith's group cut the cookies into quarters first, and passed out quarters. These are two different ways to solve the same problem. Both groups come up with three-fourths of a cookie share for each person. Three-fourths can mean one-half and one-fourth or one-fourth, one-fourth, and one-fourth." Lynne wrote on the board:

$$\frac{1}{2} + \frac{1}{4} = \frac{3}{4}$$

$$\frac{1}{4} + \frac{1}{4} + \frac{1}{4} = \frac{3}{4}$$

Lynne then gave the class an explanation of fractional symbols. "Let me explain why three-fourths is written as a 3 over a 4," she said, writing the fraction on the board. She cut a circle into four parts. "The 4 tells us that we cut the cookie into four pieces. The 3 on top tells how many pieces I have. If I have three-fourths of a cookie, I have three parts of the four parts of the whole cookie."

Lynne didn't introduce the words *numerator* and *denominator.* Instead, she used the cookies as a reference for the children. She drew on the board a diagram of what she had just done. She then asked a question that she frequently asks, "Did someone share three cookies a different way?"

Demetrius explained, "We kind of did it two ways. We gave each person a half and a quarter, but we said that also means 75 percent." He showed his group's paper.

Demetrius's group recorded several ways to share three cookies.

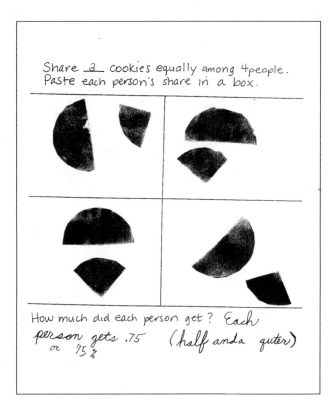

Lynne interpreted this explanation for the class. "Demetrius's group said the whole cookie is 100 percent. If you eat a whole cookie you get 100 percent of the cookie. If you eat half of a cookie, you get 50 percent. If you eat one-fourth of a cookie, you eat 25 percent. So three-fourths of a cookie is 75 percent."

Although this was the class's first formal work with fractions, it was clear that some students were familiar with the concept. Children seemed to have different pieces of information about fractions. By having the students share cookies and write and illustrate how much each person got, Lynne learned what they knew about conventional notation and how well they grasped the abstract concept of fractional parts.

Some children put chocolate chips on their cookies.

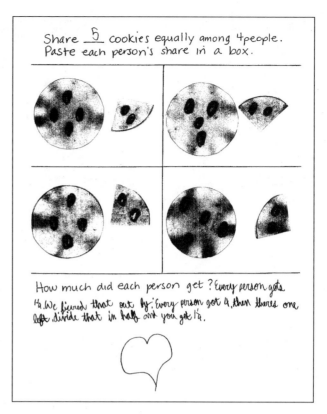

Share __5__ cookies equally among 4 people. Paste each person's share in a box.

How much did each person get? Every person gots 1¼. We figured that out by: Every person got 1, then there's one left. divide that in half and you got 1¼.

WHOLE CLASS LESSON   The Game of Leftovers

Overview

This game of chance gives children experience dividing quantities of Color Tiles into equal groups and thinking about remainders. In this lesson, the game starts with 15 tiles. Children play and discuss the game in groups. The menu activity *Leftovers with Any Number* (see page 95) extends this lesson by letting children choose any number of tiles to start the game.

Before the lesson

Gather these materials:
■ One die
■ 15 Color Tiles
■ Paper cups or other containers to hold 15 Color Tiles
■ Six small paper plates or 3-inch squares of construction paper
■ One sheet of chart paper
■ Two blank cubes, plus sticky labels for dice
■ Directions for Playing Leftovers, pages 197–198

Teaching directions

■ Tell the students that you are going to teach them how to play Leftovers, a game for partners. Show them the materials: a die, 15 Color Tiles in a cup, and six paper plates or 3-inch squares of construction paper. You may want to enlarge and post the directions, or duplicate them for each pair of students.

■ Choose a student to model a game with you. Begin by asking your student partner to count out 15 tiles. Decide who goes first.

■ The player who goes first rolls the die. This determines how many paper plates to lay out. So that the class can see what's happening in this model game, draw on the board the appropriate number of squares for each round.

■ The player who rolled the die then divides the total number of tiles in the cup into equal shares on the plates. He or she gets to keep all the leftover tiles for that round. Both players write a mathematical sentence to represent the division: for example, $15 \div 4 = 3$ R3 or $15 \div 3 = 5$ R0. During the demonstration, both you and your partner should record on the board so the others can see. (Having both players record gives all children practice with the standard notation for division. Also, while including "R0" if there is no remainder isn't conventional or essential, it is helpful to some children.)

■ Return the tiles on the plates to the cup. The second person rolls the die, takes the correct number of plates, and divides up the tiles. Both players record again.

■ Continue playing until no tiles are left. If necessary, explain to students what to do if the number of plates exceeds the number of tiles. For example, if there are four tiles and a player rolls a 6, all four tiles are leftovers. The mathematics sentence is $4 \div 6 = 0$ R4.

■ The winner is the player with the most leftovers. Check that all the leftovers total the original 15.

■ After you finish modeling the game, post the sheet of chart paper. Title it: "Division with R0" and copy below the title the sentences from the board that have remainders of zero. (Do not write duplicates.) Tell the students that after they finish a game of Leftovers they should record on the chart their sentences that have a remainder of zero. Remind them that they should check to make sure they write sentences that are not already on the chart.

■ Have students play the game in pairs. Circulate and check that they understand the rules and are playing correctly.

■ Begin class the next day with a class discussion about the game. Ask: "Which numbers were easy ones for getting remainders? Which were hard?" Students might have discovered that they get "stuck" on some numbers such as 12, for which only one number (5) has any remainders. Also, with the class, examine the class chart of division sentences with remainders of zero and have the children look for patterns. For example, looking at the sentences that begin with 10 ($10 \div 1 = 10$, $10 \div 2 = 5$, $10 \div 5 = 2$) may help children see that factors of a number can be used in two division statements. Also, children might notice that dividing by 1 produces the same answer as the number they started with.

■ Ask students to discuss the numbers they would like to have on the die if they were able to create their own.

■ Extend the game by having interested students make a new die that they think would be better for getting more leftovers. They are still limited to the numbers 1 through 6, but can eliminate some and include more duplicates of others. Have them write about the numbers they chose and why. (For a discussion about why students shouldn't put zero on a die, see page 102.)

(Note: If you don't have blank cubes for the students to use to make dice, have them cut up six squares, put a number on each square, and put them in an envelope. Removing one square from the envelope, noting the number, and then replacing it constitutes a roll of the die.)

FROM THE CLASSROOM

Lynne introduced Leftovers by reminding the children of the whole class lesson *Dividing Cookies*. "When you had an extra cookie to share," she said, "you cut it up to divide it. Who remembers how you shared five cookies among the four of you?" She wrote on the board:

Dividing Cookies

$5 \div 4 = \quad 4\overline{)5}$

Irene answered. "Everyone got one whole cookie, and then we divided the other one up," she said.

"Each person got one and one-fourth," Shannon added.

"How would I record that to complete my division sentence?" Lynne asked, pointing to what she had written on the board.

Demetrius answered, "You write a big 1 and then . . . can I come up and show?"

Lynne nodded, and Demetrius went to the board and recorded the answer in both places:

$$5 \div 4 = 1\tfrac{1}{4} \qquad 4\overline{)5}^{\,1\tfrac{1}{4}}$$

"So each person got one cookie and one-fourth of a cookie," Lynne said. "Suppose you had a problem to solve that was almost the same, but this time you had to divide up five Color Tiles among four people." The children began to talk among themselves.

"You'd have to cut them up," Ethan said.

"Yeah, you need a knife," Reggie added.

"It would be hard to cut them into pieces," Hugh said. "They're pretty small."

"You can't break them," Ashley said, a voice of practicality. "You're not supposed to."

Lynne interrupted their conversations. "Watch as I write the problem on the board. She wrote:

Dividing Color Tiles

$$5 \div 4 = \qquad 4\overline{)5}$$

"The problem looks the same, mathematically, as the *Dividing Cookies* problem," Lynne said, "but you can't cut up the Color Tiles. How could you solve it? What should I write?" The children were quiet for a moment. Then Wesley, Matthew, and Courtney raised their hands. Lynne waited a bit more to see who else might have an idea. Samantha, Demetrius, and Keith also raised their hands. Lynne called on Courtney.

"Everyone would get just one Color Tile," she said.

"That makes sense," Lynne said, "but what about the extras?"

"You'd just put it back in the box," Matthew suggested.

"You could do that," Lynne said, "but watch as I show you how to record mathematically when there is a leftover." She completed the recordings on the board:

$$5 \div 4 = 1 \text{ R1} \qquad 4\overline{)5}^{\,1\,\text{R1}}$$

"The first 1 tells that each person gets one Color Tile, just like the 1 told that each person got one cookie," Lynne explained. "Then the R1 tells that there is one extra that's left over. The R stands for 'remainder,' and we say 'remainder 1.' The answer is 1 remainder 1."

Lynne then posed another problem. "What if you were going to divide five Color Tiles among three people, instead of four people," she said. "Talk with your neighbor about what I could write to show the answer mathematically."

Some of the children used their fingers to figure out the answer. Reggie, sitting near the Color Tiles, grabbed five of them to help him think. In a few moments, Lynne called the children back to attention.

"Who can tell me what to write?" she asked. Almost half the students raised their hands. Lynne called on Ethan.

"It's 1 remainder 2," he said, confidently.

"I'll record," Lynne said, and wrote:

$$5 \div 3 = 1\,R2 \qquad 3\overline{)5}^{\,1\,R2}$$

To make sure the others understood, Lynne drew on the board three stick figures and five squares to represent the three people and the five Color Tiles. "I can give each person one Color Tile," she explained, drawing a line from each stick figure to a square. "Then there are two leftovers, the remainder," she said, circling the two extra squares.

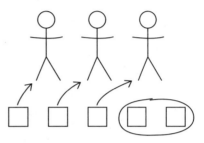

Lynne then introduced the children to the game. "Now I'm going to teach you how to play a game called Leftovers," she began. "It's a game of chance for partners and uses remainders. The winner is the person who gets more leftovers. I'm going to play the game with Irene, so you can see the way it works." Irene came up and joined Lynne at the board.

Lynne cautioned the class, "The game isn't hard to play, but you have to count carefully and keep careful records."

Lynne picked up a plastic cup containing tiles. "Your first job is to make sure you have 15 tiles. Irene, will you make sure we have 15?" Irene counted the tiles and nodded her head.

"Also, you need a die and six squares of paper like this," Lynne said, showing these items to the children. "We'll call these squares `plates.' You go first," Lynne said to Irene. "Roll the die."

Irene rolled a 4.

"The die tells you how many paper plates to lay out," Lynne explained. "Irene, you lay out four plates and put the others aside for now. I'll draw four plates on the board so everyone can see.

"Next, the person who rolled the die takes the Color Tiles and divides them up so there's the same number on each plate," Lynne explained.

Irene began to share the tiles. (Some of the children watched Irene divide the tiles; others tried to figure out how many to put on each square.) Irene first put two tiles on each. She tried counting what was left in the cup, but abandoned that idea and put one more tile on each plate. "There aren't enough to go around again," Irene said. "There are three left over."

To illustrate what Irene had done, Lynne drew on the board three tiles in each of the four squares and drew the three leftovers separately.

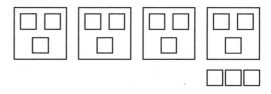

"Next, both people record the division sentence. You'll record on paper, but Irene and I will record on the board. I'll do it first. We'll record just one way for this game." Lynne wrote the equation: *15 ÷ 4 = 3 R3.* Then she wrote the letter I in front of it:

$$I \ 15 \div 4 = 3 \ R3$$

"This *I* will help me remember that Irene rolled the die," Lynne explained. Lynne designated a place on the board for Irene to record, and Irene copied what Lynne had written.

"Irene rolled the die, so she gets to keep the three leftovers and put the rest back in the cup," Lynne said. "How many tiles do we have now?"

"Fifteen!" exclaimed Reggie.

"We have 15 altogether," Lynne said, "but how many are in the cup now that Irene got to keep the 3 left over?" Irene counted and reported 12 tiles.

"Now it's my turn to roll the die," Lynne said. She rolled a 6, put out six paper plates, and drew six squares on the board. "I have to divide the 12 tiles among the six squares," Lynne said. She did this quickly and then drew on the board two tiles in each of the six squares.

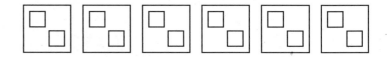

"There's nothing left over," Brittany said.

"That's right," Lynne said. "Who can tell us what to write?" She called on Amari, and she and Irene recorded as Amari dictated:

$$12 \div 6 = 2 \ R0$$

Then she added a Z in front to indicate that it had been her roll.

"There was no remainder, so do I get to keep any tiles?" Lynne asked.

"No," chorused the class.

"That's right," she said. "So, how many tiles do we have now?"

"Twelve," they answered. Lynne put the 12 tiles back into the cup.

Next, Irene rolled a 5. She put out five plates and divided the tiles as Lynne drew on the board. Aaron dictated the equation, and Lynne and Irene both recorded:

$$I \ 12 \div 5 = 2 \ R2$$

"Irene's winning," Samantha giggled. "She's lucky."

Lynne and Irene continued to play the game, recording the plays on the board. The final list of equations was:

I	$15 \div 4 = 3 \text{ R}3$
Z	$12 \div 6 = 2 \text{ R}0$
I	$12 \div 5 = 2 \text{ R}2$
Z	$10 \div 3 = 3 \text{ R}1$
I	$9 \div 3 = 3 \text{ R}0$
Z	$9 \div 6 = 1 \text{ R}3$
I	$6 \div 3 = 2 \text{ R}0$
Z	$6 \div 3 = 2 \text{ R}0$
I	$6 \div 6 = 1 \text{ R}0$
Z	$6 \div 4 = 1 \text{ R}2$
I	$4 \div 5 = 0 \text{ R}4$

"The last one is neat," Demetrius said. "Irene got to keep all four."

"She got stuck on 6, though," Brenna said. "I bet you can get stuck forever."

"Not forever," Calie corrected. "Something has to happen."

"Maybe not," Brenna insisted.

"Who won?" Truc wanted to know.

"Let's count our tiles," Lynne said. Irene reported she had nine and Lynne reported six.

"Do we have all 15 together?" Lynne asked. Irene counted the tiles; others figured in their heads or used their fingers.

"There's one more thing you and your partner have to do before you start another game," Lynne said. "Listen and watch, please." Lynne posted a large sheet of chart paper and titled it "Division with R0."

"On this chart, write all the sentences from your papers that have a remainder of zero," Lynne instructed. "But don't write the same one twice, like $6 \div 3 = 2 \text{ R}0$."

As the children read the sentences on the board, Lynne recorded the four different sentences that had remainders of zero.

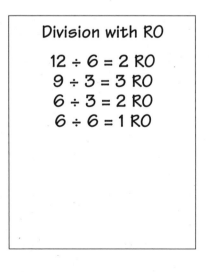

Division with R0

$12 \div 6 = 2 \text{ R}0$

$9 \div 3 = 3 \text{ R}0$

$6 \div 3 = 2 \text{ R}0$

$6 \div 6 = 1 \text{ R}0$

"When you record your sentences on the chart," Lynne said, "don't add any that Irene and I already wrote. Just new ones."

Observing the Children

The students returned to their tables to work with their partners. Hugh, acknowledged by his peers as the class clown, spent his time building a tower out of tiles. He invited Ethan, acknowledged by his peers as an all-star writer and math whiz, to blow it down. Ethan grinned and blew. Then Ethan built a tower for Hugh to blow down.

Tomfoolery out of the way, they began to play Leftovers. Ethan rolled 3 and wrote: $15 \div 3 = 5$ *R0*. Hugh copied it. Ethan didn't bother to use the construction-paper squares. Hugh didn't use them either; Ethan gave him the answers.

Tano and Kent ran into difficulties immediately. Kent rolled a 1, and Tano wrote the equation without using the paper squares: *15 ÷ 1 = 0.* Lynne spotted the equation and said to Kent, "The paper squares are your plates. The die tells you how many plates to lay out."

"One plate," said Kent.

"Now you divide the tiles equally on however many plates you have," directed Lynne.

"Fifteen?" asked Kent, his tone indicating disbelief.

"If there is one person and 15 cookies and he gets all of them, how many cookies will he get?" Lynne asked.

Kent was astounded and pleased, not at all worried that he didn't get any leftovers.

Shannon was playing with Veronica. Veronica had gone first, rolled a 2, and had 1 tile left over from the 15. With 14 left, Shannon rolled a 5, put out five plates, and both girls recorded: *14 ÷ 5 = .* As Shannon began to divide up the tiles, Veronica punched the numbers into the calculator and said, "The answer is 28." She started to write it down.

"It can't be," protested Shannon. "We don't have 28 tiles." She punched numbers into the calculator. "It's 2.8."

They didn't know what that meant and went to get Lynne. "You have to count out the tiles on the squares to find out how many leftovers you have," Lynne explained.

Shannon did this. "Four," she said, holding up the cup containing the extra four tiles. She took the extras and picked up the tiles on the plates and returned them to the cup.

Lynne said, "For this game, the calculator won't help. It figures the problem as if you were dividing cookies, not tiles. How many tiles will you be working with now?"

Shannon tried counting by eyeballing the tiles in the cup. After a few tries, she gave up, dumped the the tiles on the table, and counted. "Ten," she concluded.

Veronica wasn't paying attention. She was anxious to roll the die. "I got 4."

Shannon wrote: *10 ÷ 4 = .* She put out four paper plates. Veronica dealt out two tiles for each plate. She was excited because she had two left over.

Lynne interjected, "Can you give every plate another cube?"

Veronica looked confused. "You can't," Shannon said; "you don't have enough. Let's write." Veronica followed Shannon's lead and both girls recorded: *10 ÷ 4 = 2 R2.*

"How many tiles do you have for the next round?" asked Lynne.

Shannon transferred the tiles from the paper squares to the plastic cup, counting as she did so. "Eight," she said. She rolled the die and wrote:

8 ÷ 3 = 2 R2. She did this by herself, with no help from Lynne or Veronica. Then she told Veronica, "Copy this. Then you'll start with 6." This time she didn't count the tiles. "I just know," she explained.

Lynne circulated among the groups, sitting with one group for a few minutes and then moving on to another. When children wanted to rush through the game, she tried to slow them down, encouraging them to be methodical. Lynne showed them the importance of laying out the paper plates and counting the tiles they had at the start of each round. When children skipped steps, they got into trouble and the game didn't work out.

Matthew and Irene were typical of children who didn't quite understand the activity when they started. Both confident of their mathematical ability, both valuing speed, they didn't share their tiles on the paper squares and did not count the tiles at the beginning of each round. They relied on thinking they knew the right answers to division problems. Lynne scanned their paper.

"You've made two errors," she told them.

"Where?" Matthew demanded to know.

"You can find them if you replay the game," Lynne said. She sat with them as they got started.

Lynne noticed two errors and asked Matthew and Irene to replay the game.

Leftovers with
15

M.B
$15 \div 3 = 5 \, R0$
$14 \div 4 = 3 \, R3 \quad \leftarrow$
$9 \div 1 = 9 \, R0$
$9 \div 4 = 2 \, R1$
$8 \div 1 = 8 \, R0$
$8 \div 3 = 2 \, R2$
$4 \div 6 = 0 \, R4$

I.Y.
$13 \div 2 = 7 \, R1$
$11 \div 5 = 2 \, R1$
$9 \div 3 = 3 \, R0$
$8 \div 2 = 4 \, R0$
$8 \div 4 = 2 \, R0$
$6 \div 5 = 5 \, R1 \quad \leftarrow$
$5 \div 2 = 2 \, R1$

Winner (10)   Loser 5

When Matthew found the error he had made dividing 14 into four groups, he said, "Oh, no. Then it all changes from here." Lynne agreed and reminded them to slow down, lay out squares according to the roll of the die, count leftovers, and then count the tiles for the next round. She left them to redo the rest of their game.

Lynne noticed that Ashley and Jamie had written *9 ÷ 4 = 2 with R2.* When Lynne questioned that answer, the girls said they got the answer by counting tiles on the paper squares. Lynne asked them to do it again so she could see. It turned out they had 10 tiles, not 9. Lynne explained that mistaking the number of tiles at the beginning throws off the whole game. "Also," she told them, "you don't need to write *with*." The girls fixed their papers.

Lynne noted that Kent and Tano were now off to a good start in their game, but she spotted a glitch on the seventh move. "Replay 10 divided by 5," she requested.

"It's 2 and no remainder," reported Tano.

"Right. But look at what you wrote here," she pointed out. She asked the boys to replay their game from that point on.

This game was completed in 10 rounds.

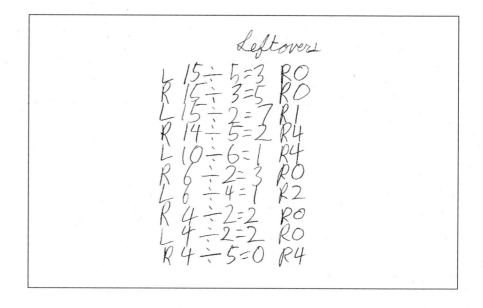

A Class Discussion

The next day, Lynne called the class to the floor at the front of the room. "Leftovers is a division game that can show us some interesting things about numbers," she began. "When you played Leftovers, what was a very hard number to get out of?"

Demetrius and Wesley exclaimed together, "Twelve! It's impossible."

Lynne copied onto the board division sentences from the class chart that began with 12:

$$12 \div 1 = 12 \text{ RO}$$
$$12 \div 3 = 4 \text{ RO}$$
$$12 \div 6 = 2 \text{ RO}$$
$$12 \div 2 = 6 \text{ RO}$$
$$12 \div 4 = 3 \text{ RO}$$

"Now there's only one more thing to throw," she commented.

"Five!" offered the class.

Lynne added: *12 ÷ 5 =* to the list on the board.

"What happens with this number?" she asked.

"It's 2 remainder 2," Matthew said.

"Wow!" Demetrius said. "Every number on the die except 5 comes out even, with no remainders. That's what makes it so hard. You need remainders for the game to work."

"Who had another number besides 12 that was hard to get out of?" asked Lynne.

"Six," replied Truc.

"Can you explain why?" asked Lynne.

"Every number on the die comes out even except for 4 and 5," explained Truc.

Lynne suggested that the children check the class chart for sentences that began with 6.

"What other discoveries did you make about Leftovers?" asked Lynne.

"You don't get remainders a lot when you roll a 2," Amari said.

"Let's look at the chart," Lynne said.

"It works for 6, 10, 8, 14 . . . ," Aaron read from the chart.

"Hey, those are all even," Irene noticed.

"Of course," Matthew said, "an even number always splits into two."

"Fourteen is a good number," offered Reggie.

"Why is that?" asked Lynne.

"You usually get something," Reggie grinned.

Demetrius and Wesley found that 12 was a hard number to move beyond.

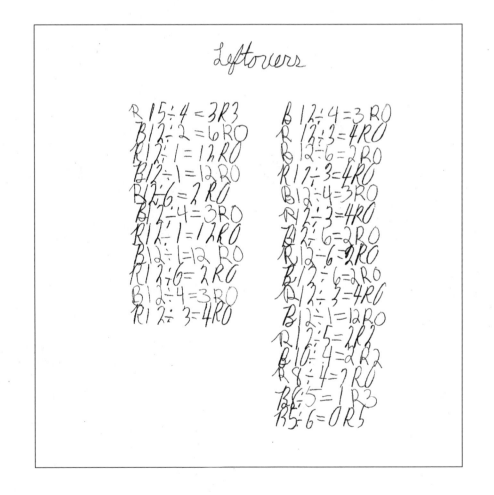

A Lesson Extension

Lynne then posed a question that led to an extension of the game. "Suppose you made your own die for the game," she said. "What numbers would you put on it?"

"One is a very unlucky number," offered Patricia.

"I agree," responded Lynne. "Why do you think it's unlucky?"

"Because there are never leftovers," said Patricia.

"If you took 1 off the die, what would you put on?" Lynne asked.

"Seven," suggested Wesley.

"We don't have seven plates," explained Lynne. "What number would you repeat on the die?"

"I would have 2, 3, 4, 5, and another 3 and 2," Ethan said.

Brittany suggested putting all 6s on her die. Lynne responded, "If you have all the same number, then you wouldn't have to even roll the die because it would always come up the same." Brittany decided to put four 6s and two 1s on her die.

"But if you have 6s you get stuck forever on 12 because 12 divided by 6 is 2," said Kent.

"How many agree with Kent about the 6? Is it lucky or unlucky?" Lynne asked.

"I don't like it because I always get stuck on it," said Keith.

"Courtney, what die would you make?" asked Lynne.

"I think 2, 2, 3, 3, 4, 4 would be good," she said.

"How come?" asked Lynne.

Courtney shrugged. "I just think so," she said. "They were good for me."

Lynne said to the class, "Today you can play Leftovers with a regular die, or you can make your own die. I have blank cubes and sticky labels for you to use. But if you make your own die, I need to know why you made it the way you did. So write down what numbers you chose and why."

Shannon asked, "Can your partner have different numbers?"

"Yes," Lynne answered, "you can decide whether you want to make two dice or share one."

Ethan and Hugh spent a good deal of time arguing about how to make their dice. Ethan was adamant that Hugh not put a 6 on his die. Finally, Ethan decided to make his own die. "I'm going to put three 5s on my die, so if I get 12 I can get past it easier."

Ethan explained why he included three 5s on his die.

New Die For Leftovers

On my die I put 3 fives I put them on because 5 is the only way to get out of 12. I put a 2 because it gets out of any odd number. I had 2 spaces left so I put on a 3 and a 2 and a 4.

Samantha recommended making a die with "good numbers."

> I picked 5,4,2, 6,5, 3, because those numbers are more possible then, the others like 1, 1 well have 1 pile. and you well never have remainders. I recommend if you make your one dice you good numbers.

Kyle explains the discovery he made about rolling a 1.

> Left overs with 30
>
> I picked 3, 2, 4, 5 and another 2 and 4 because you wouldn't get stuck with those numbers. as much I didn't pick one and six because you would get stuck on these number I always get stuck on one.

WHOLE CLASS LESSON   Explorations with Raisins

Overview

In this whole class lesson, students investigate small snack boxes of raisins and explore numbers and division in ways that reach beyond computation and conventional word problems by emphasizing thinking and reasoning. In the course of the lesson, students apply whole number operations, estimate, consider statistical ideas, think about measurements of volume and weight, and make proportional comparisons. The menu activity *Raisins in the Big Box* (see page 109) continues students' experiences with estimating, counting, and dividing.

Before the lesson

Gather these materials:
■ $\frac{1}{2}$-ounce boxes of raisins, one per child
■ One sheet of chart paper

Teaching directions

■ Ask the children to clear their desks, and give each child a box of raisins. Assure the children they will get to eat the raisins but stress the importance of waiting until they complete their investigations.

■ Ask the children to guess how many raisins are in their boxes. Record their guesses, identify the smallest and largest, and, if you wish, talk about the range.

■ Demonstrate opening the top of the raisin box and looking at the visible raisins, emphasizing that each student will write an estimate of how many raisins are in his or her box before removing them to count.

■ Invite children to empty their raisins out onto sheets of paper. Ask them to group their raisins in some way so you can count them quickly as you walk by.

■ On a chart at the front of the room record how many raisins each child reports and lead a general discussion about the results.

FROM THE CLASSROOM

"Today we're going to share raisins," Lynne said to the class. "And these will be real raisins, not pretend like the cookies. So once you finish the mathematics of sharing raisins, you can eat them."

Lynne then explained to the students that to get ready for this activity they needed to clear off their desks. "The only thing on your desk should be a box of raisins, two sheets of paper, and a pencil." Eager to find out what raisins had to do with mathematics, the children cleared their desks quickly. As they did so, Lynne distributed a $\frac{1}{2}$-ounce box of raisins to each child. Also, she gave each child a sheet of lined paper and a sheet of unlined yellow copier paper.

"Here is how you should label your lined papers," she said, as she wrote on the board:

Name
Raisin Explorations

Reggie, always eager to anticipate directions, announced, "I know what we have to do. We have to subtract."

Lynne held up a small box of raisins. "Think about this box of raisins. Without opening your box, guess how many raisins you think are inside."

After a few moments, Lynne asked the children to report their guesses. "Don't worry about what others think," she said. "These are only guesses, and you can always change your guess when you have more information."

Most of the students were eager to offer estimates. Numbers came as quickly as Lynne could write them on the board:

33   13   30   10   16   31   20   12   33

Lynne stood back and looked at what she had written. She asked, "Does anyone think there are more than 33 raisins?"

Matthew obliged, "34," and Brittany quickly offered, "41."

Lynne continued taking estimates until all who wanted to report had the chance to do so. She continued to write the estimates on the board. Then she asked the children, "What is the range of our estimates?"

To explain this new term, Lynne said, "To find a range, look for the lowest number and the highest number. And when you report a range you subtract the lowest number from the highest. Would someone like to report our range?" Lynne used correct statistical terminology, knowing that her students enjoy trying out new vocabulary and that they'll become familiar with such terms as they reappear in working contexts.

Aaron was eager to demonstrate his understanding of this new concept and volunteered, "The range is 10 and 41, that's 31," he said.

"We say the range of our estimates is 31," Lynne said, again using the terminology correctly. "Does anyone think there are fewer than 10 raisins?" No one responded.

"It can't be," Irene finally offered, "because raisins are small."

Carey said, "If there was 41, it would have to be a bigger box."

"Mrs. Zolli, can I use a ruler to find out how long the box is?" asked Ethan, holding up his ruler.

"Sure, and tell us," Lynne responded.

"It's about 2 inches high," said Ethan.

"And this way?" asked Lynne, pointing to the width of the box.

Ethan measured. "It's $1\frac{1}{2}$ inches," he reported.

"And this way?" Lynne pointed to the depth of the top of the box. "Remember, there are three ways to measure."

"It's $\frac{3}{4}$ of an inch," he said.

"Do you think the company puts the exact same number of raisins in every box?" asked Lynne.

The class immediately chorused, "NO!"

"But in packages of Lifesavers, there are always 10 Lifesavers," said Lynne.

"No, 11," three students immediately corrected her, indicating social information for which students are more expert than teachers.

"They just stuff raisins in," said Keith. "They don't count them."

Lynne pointed out that sometimes products are packaged by weight, not number. She wrote on the board:

Net weight $\frac{1}{2}$ oz.

"'Net weight' means that's what the raisins weigh without counting them," she explained. "Find this information on your box," she said.

Aaron read aloud, "One and a half ounces."

"It says '$\frac{1}{2}$ ounce,'" Lynne said gently to Aaron. "If it were $1\frac{1}{2}$ ounces, it would have to have a 1 in front, like this." She wrote $1\frac{1}{2}$ on the board. Aaron nodded. "We'll be using boxes that size later on the menu," Lynne added.

"Did anyone find other weights on the box?" Lynne then asked.

"I see 14.1 grams," volunteered Brenna.

"The company weighs $\frac{1}{2}$ ounce or 14.1 grams of raisins, which are the same weight, and then puts them into the box," Lynne explained. "Think about this: If you have big raisins in your box, will you have more or fewer raisins than if you have small raisins?"

A half dozen children responded quickly: "Less." A few responded "More" just as quickly. A conversation broke out among the students. In a few moments, all were in agreement that there would be fewer raisins in the box if they were bigger.

Lynne continued, "All of you have made guesses about the number of raisins in this box. In just a moment, you'll open the top of your box and look inside. Listen carefully first. Don't touch the raisins; just look carefully at the ones on top. Then think to yourself about how many you estimate there are in all—and why. Don't talk with others yet; you'll have a chance to share your estimates in a bit. For now, think and record on your paper." Lynne wrote on the board:

> After opening the box my estimate is _____.
> I think this because _____.

When the students opened their boxes, some stared for a bit at the top layer; some immediately started counting the visible raisins; others tried to count layers, using their fingers to measure. After she noticed that all of the students had recorded, Lynne had them report their estimates and reasons.

"I thought there were 10, but now I see there are more," Ashley said. "They're more squished up than I thought."

Ashley revised her estimate from 10 to 40.

Raisin Exploration

My estimate is __10__ raisins.

My esimate after opening the box is __40__

I think this because at first I thought that there would be 10. Then I counted just the top row, and there were already 8. There is a lot more rows than just 1 row so I chang my guess to 40.

Courtney thought there were 20 raisins in her box "because they don't come all the way to the top," she reported.

Kent guessed 31. "I still think 31," he said, "because I counted 10 and I think there's space for two more 10s and an extra."

Kent didn't change his first estimate of 31.

After opening the box my estimate is still 31.
I think this because I counted 10 raisins and it only took this much room [   ] and if I did that 3 times that equals 30 plus 1 extra makes 31.

| 10 |
| 10 |
| 10 |

Demetrius estimated 22. "I looked at the top, and I found 7, and then I measured how high the box was . . . and counted 7, 8, 9, 10 . . . "

Keith guessed 30 and explained, "I tried 15 and then I doubled it."

"I'll guess 25," Reggie said. "That's more than I thought before." When Lynne asked him to explain his reasoning, Reggie insisted, "I just know there's more."

Some children reported how they used layers to come up with estimates. Shannon said, "I counted six, and I think there are six layers and some extra, so I changed to 38."

Matthew said, "I thought 10, but I can see 7 on top, and it looks like there's 7 down. But I don't think there's 7 in each row. I guess 46."

Matthew thought his box had seven layers with seven or fewer raisins in each layer. He estimated 46.

Raisin Explorations

After opening the box my estimate is 46 I think think this because theres 7 on the top and it looks like 7 down but I don't think theres 7 in each row.

After the children had the opportunity to report their estimates, Lynne asked, "Is there anybody who thinks there are fewer than 20?"

"I say 16," smiled Truc.

"How many think there are more than 20 raisins?" asked Lynne. Most of the hands went up. "More than 30?" she asked, upping the ante.

Justine wanted to backtrack. "I think there are more than 22 but less than 30; I think there are 29."

"There are 33!" exclaimed Hugh.

"What did you think before?" asked Lynne.

"I thought 13," Hugh said. "But that was before I looked."

"You've increased your estimate because you have more information now," Lynne commented, offering students the rationale for changing their guesses.

"I guess 40," said Ethan, "because my raisins are really small."

"How many are on your top layer, Ethan?" asked Lynne, prompting him to think about his reason a different way.

"Six," he responded.

"How many layers do you think are in the box?" Lynne pressed.

Ethan looked closely at his box. "Ten? No, maybe 6," he said. He thought a moment and said, "And 6 times 6 equals 36, so I think there are 36 raisins in my box." He changed his estimate on his paper.

"I think there are 20," offered Garrett, grinning. "I opened both ends and guessed at the middle."

Counting the Raisins

"Put your boxes down now and look at me," Lynne instructed, to get the students' attention. "Next, you'll count your raisins. That's what the yellow paper is for, so you can dump out your raisins and count them. But don't eat any yet." Some children laughed. Lynne added, "We *will* eat the raisins, but please wait so that we can do some more mathematics first.

"Group your raisins in a way so that as I come around I can quickly see how many you have," Lynne added. "Once you've decided how to group your raisins, circle each group, drawing the raisins or writing the number in each circle. That way, when you take the raisins away there will still be a picture of how many raisins you had to start with.

"Okay, go ahead. Dump out your raisins and represent them on your paper."

The students began excitedly. Several of them had trouble getting all the raisins out of their boxes because they stuck together. Lynne suggested that they open both ends of the box and try pushing them out.

Each child concentrated intently on his or her own box of raisins. "I have a lot of raisins!" exclaimed Truc. Garrett, who exhibits little number savvy, carefully counted one by one. Across the room, Matthew also counted one by one. When Irene told him, "It's quicker if you group them," Matthew grouped by 5s, but he couldn't seem to figure out how to use the groupings to determine how many he had altogether.

Irene lined up her raisins in horizontal rows of 10s. Once she had four rows, she commented, "My estimate was way off."

Irene grouped by 10s; she had four 10s and four extra raisins.

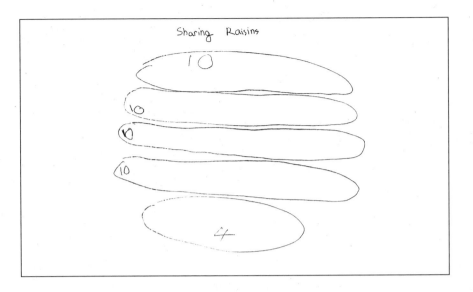

Many children grouped their raisins by 2s—but in different ways. Hugh counted out loud by 2s as he put his raisins into groups of two. Justine and Kent grouped their raisins the same way.

Kent put 37 raisins into groups of 2.

Cynthia, however, put all of her raisins on one side of the paper and moved them, two by two, into a pile on the other side, counting by 2s as she did so. Samantha and Ashley did this as well. Samantha got mixed up in the middle and had to start again. When she noticed what Justine had done, she began arranging her raisins into groups of two.

Brittany arranged her raisins into groups of five. Shannon, who has difficulty with numbers, watched Brittany make one group of five and began to group her own raisins the same way.

Seven children grouped by 2s, nine grouped by 5s, and ten grouped by 10s. Demetrius grouped by 3s and Carey by 4s. Courtney grouped 25 of her raisins by 5s and then switched to 3s. She wrote: *I have thirty-three,* but she pictured 43. She saw her error and erased two groups of five.

Courtney started grouping by 5s, then switched to 3s.

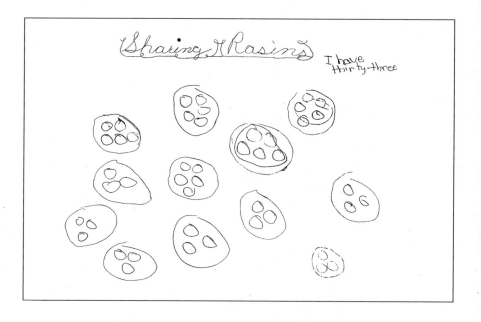

Lynne learned about her students by watching how they grouped their raisins to count them and then how they handled recording their data. She noted that Hugh, who often seems so disorganized, was very orderly in drawing and counting his raisin groups. "He counted by 2s, but he kept track of things."

Matthew, who knows his math facts, was in real trouble. He didn't seem to keep track of anything. Lynne suspected that the problem was not that he couldn't do it but that he tends to be easily distracted, easily "bored." Lynne keeps a close eye on Matthew to help him complete assignments.

A Class Discussion

Once the students had recorded their raisin groups, Lynne called them to the front of the room. "Bring your yellow papers," she said. She had posted a large sheet of chart paper.

When the children were seated, Lynne said, "I'm going to record your counts. I wonder who has the smallest number of raisins. Does anybody have less than 33? 31?" She wrote 31 to begin the chart. Then, as students reported their totals, she added the numbers to the chart.

"Now, when I call your number," Lynne said, "tell us how you grouped your raisins." Lynne started with Cynthia, who had counted 31.

"I did it by 10s," she said.

"How many groups of 10 and how many extras?" Lynne asked.

"Three 10s and one extra," Cynthia replied.

"That's three groups of 10 and 1 left over," Lynne said to model for the others how to report. As students reported, Lynne recorded the data:

31:    3 groups of 10 and 1 left over
32:    6 groups of 5 and 2 left over
32:    3 groups of 10 and 2 left over
33:    3 groups of 10 and 3 left over
33:    6 groups of 5 and 3 left over
34:    3 groups of 10 and 4 left over
34:    17 groups of 2s
35:    8 groups of 4 and 3 left over
35:    7 groups of 5
36:    12 groups of 3
36:    12 groups of 3
36:    3 groups of 10 and 6 left over
36:    3 groups of 10 and 6 left over
37:    7 groups of 5 and 2 left over
37:    5 groups of 7 and 2 left over

When Lynne wrote the two descriptions for 37, Reggie excitedly exclaimed, "Hey! There's two different ways: 7 groups of 5 or 5 groups of 7—both with 2 left over. It's the same thing." Lynne smiled, and the students continued reporting. They were interested in the counts and how their classmates had grouped raisins to get them.

37:    18 groups of 2 and 1 left over
37:    3 groups of 10 and 7 left over
38:    18 groups of 2

"You'd better count again," protested Ashley. "I had the same method, and I have 19 groups of 2."
"Oops, I skipped a number. It's 19 groups of 2," agreed Hugh.

38:    3 groups of 10 and 8 left over
38:    7 groups of 5 and 3 left over
39:    3 groups of 10 and 9 left over
39:    3 groups of 10 and 9 left over
39:    7 groups of 5 and 4 left over

When Lynne reached 40, Garrett reported, "By 5s."
"Count how many groups," instructed Lynne.
Garrett counted what he had drawn. "Eight groups of 5," he said.

40:    8 groups of 5
40:    20 groups of 2
40:    4 groups of 10
44:    4 groups of 10 and 4 left over

Lynne invited the class to look at these statistics. She acknowledged the many different ways students had found to group their raisins.

"What's the range of our actual counts?" Lynne asked.

Courtney responded, "It's 12, no 13. It's 13."

"How did you figure?" Lynne wanted to know.

"I went 31 . . . 41, then 42, 43, 44. That's 10 and 3 more," she said.

"The range of our counts is much smaller than the range of our estimates," Lynne said. "That's because we had real information, not just guesses."

Then Lynne held up an unopened box and asked, "If I were going to guess how many raisins were in this box, what would be a good guess?"

"Forty!" exclaimed Reggie.

"Explain your thinking," prodded Lynne.

"That's how many I had," he said.

"Thirty-five," offered Samantha. "Look at the chart. Most people got that number."

"But lots more people got more than 35," observed Aaron. "I think 37 or 38 would be a better guess."

Lynne chose not to go into the formal idea of averaging but noted the children's intuitive explanations.

Group Combining and Sharing

Lynne then announced, "You need to work together in groups for the next two problems. First, you need to decide how many raisins your table has altogether and write about how you reached that decision. Then you need to share the raisins equally among your group." She distributed one sheet of paper to each group, saying, "On your papers, you'll report how many raisins each person got and explain how you did the sharing."

The children responded eagerly to this task. Their approaches varied widely. Shannon immediately started counting everybody's raisins one by one. Courtney and Jamie wrote down each person's total and used a calculator to find the grand total. In another group, Ethan and Aaron recorded each person's total and added, using paper and pencil. Irene did the same for her group. Cynthia, Calie, Garrett, and Kent dumped their raisins in the center of the table and then, in turn, began taking raisins one by one. Vivian and Justine talked about what they should do, but Reggie exclaimed, "I'm the champion! I have 40." He started eating.

Vivian protested to Lynne, "He's eating them."

"All he does is argue with us," added Justine. Wesley, the fourth member of the group, silently started adding the totals.

"Did you eat raisins?" asked Lynne. When Reggie denied doing so, she advised the group, "Tell him what to do. When you work in groups you must keep group members advised of what they need to do."

"We need to take turns," Vivian said to Reggie. "Everybody take a raisin." They each took a raisin from the center, and then another.

"Could you do it in a faster way?" asked Lynne. No one answered. "How about 10? Could you each take 10 raisins?"

Justine grinned, and instructed her teammates, "Everybody take 10!"

In her group, Jamie tried to convince Wesley, who had the most (40), to give 2 raisins to the person with the least (35). She tried to explain, but Wesley didn't see why he should give away 2 if nobody else at the table was giving away any. They decided to use the calculator and divide their total by 4. When the calculator showed 35.5 they didn't know what to do. After some discussion, they decided to push all the raisins into the center and dole them out one by one.

Lynne returned to Irene's group and asked, "So how many did your group end up getting?"

"We can't figure it out," Brittany said.

"What happened?" Lynne asked.

Irene said, "I don't know," and laughed.

"Do you have a total?" persisted Lynne.

"Yeah, it's 149," replied Irene.

"What happens next?" Lynne probed.

Matthew offered, "First, we're going to try figuring it out. Maybe we should put them all together and then pass them out and see what we get."

"We tried the calculator," Brenna explained for her group. "We added all our raisins and got the answer. Then we divided by 4, but it didn't work. It's 37.25."

The group agreed to stay in with Lynne during recess and figure out this problem. But they spent a lot of time arguing over who would draw raisins first from the center pile. Finally, Lynne insisted that they needed to finish. "You have 10 minutes," she warned. The students explained that they wanted to take 10 each but couldn't decide who should go first. They liked Lynne's suggestion that they take simultaneously. Each child took 10, 10, 10, 5. Three raisins were left over. They gave the extras to Lynne. "That will save more argument," said Irene.

Then they worked on writing their solution. The math was not quite right, but the children had persevered with a difficult division problem, in the process discovering something about division, something about the benefits and liabilities of the calculator, and something about group process.

Aaron, Ethan, Keith, and Hugh used a calculator successfully to help them divide their raisins. They weren't stumped when the answer appeared as 37.25. They reported that each person would get *37 and a qutar,* deciding ¼ raisin is possible mathematically, if not in the real world. "You wouldn't really divide a raisin into quarters," explained Aaron, "but you can write ¼ anyway."

Kyle, Tano, and Truc comprised a group of three. Once they had added their raisins, they noticed that they could simplify the division by first giving everybody 30. Then they had 12 left over. At this point, they ran into trouble and said that each person would get 2 out of the 12. By now, everyone was eating raisins, and no one noticed that the shares were not equal.

Kyle, Tano, and Truc did not notice their mathematical error.

$$
\begin{array}{r}
33 \\
33 \\
+36 \\
\hline
102
\end{array}
$$

We added 33, 33, and 36 together and we got 102.

Each person got 30 because that equal 90 and 12 are leftover and each person got 2 and that makes 102.

When Garrett was asked what he thought of this activity, he was enthusiastic. "I got to tell the class what our group did. I reported for our group. And I liked trying to help other people. My partner next to me said he had trouble counting out the raisins, so I helped." Garrett grinned, "And in the end I ate my math."

As the math period ended, Lynne decided to introduce the class to one more "number sense" activity. "How many raisins did we eat today? More than 100?"

"Yes!" responded the children.

"More than 1,000?" The children were doubtful. A hum of murmuring spread through the room, but no one volunteered.

"More than a million?" asked Lynne.

"Noooo." The children were sure of themselves, certain that a million was too many.

"How many do you suppose we did eat? Does anyone have a guess?" Truc's guess sounded tentative. "Maybe 695?"

"I say 700." Courtney was more positive.

"I bet it's 175," Reggie said confidently.

"Let's see," suggested Lynne. "What about for six people? How many would six people get altogether?" Justine used a calculator to multiply 6 by 36 and figured that six children might receive 216 raisins. Lynne wrote this number on the board.

"Do you want to change your guess for 30 children?" No one responded. Lynne suggested that students might use the chart to find out how many raisins the class ate. Reggie rushed to the front of the room with a calculator, entered some numbers, and then turned to the group and reported, "It's going to be a very, very high number."

Esme, Juliette, Robin, and Patricia worked to make sense of the numbers.

> ## Raisin Problem
> The total for our whole table is 121. The next even number is 122. Half of 122 is 61 make that 60½. The next even number is 60. Half of 60 is 30. Make it 30¼. Everybody gets 30¼. The remainder is 1.

CONTENTS

The Doorbell Rings Again   89
Leftovers with Any Number   95
Raisins in the Big Box   109
Candy Box Family Guides   116
17 Kings and 42 Elephants   135
Sharing Candy Bars   145
Hungry Ants   157
Division Stories   167

MENU ACTIVITIES

The eight activities on the menu were chosen to offer children a variety of ways to think about division. The menu was constructed with the consideration that not all children get the same benefits from the same experiences. The menu includes activities that can be understood at different levels and activities that appeal to varied interests and aptitudes. Although you can require students to do all the assigned work, know that they will respond differently to the activities. This is to be expected and respected.

Three of the menu activities extend whole class lessons. *The Doorbell Rings Again* is based on the whole class lesson *The Doorbell Rang* and gives children the opportunity to invent their own sharing stories. *Leftovers with Any Number* extends the *Leftovers* whole class lesson and allows children to choose the number of Color Tiles they'll use. In *Raisins in the Big Box,* an extension of the *Explorations with Raisins* whole class lesson, children estimate, count, and divide the raisins in a $1^1/_2$-ounce box.

Candy Box Family Guides is an extension of the *Candy Box* whole class lesson and menu activity from the replacement unit *Math By All Means: Multiplication, Grade 3.* (See the Bibliography on page 209.) However, children can benefit from the activity even if they haven't had the experience from the multiplication unit.

Two other menu activities, *17 Kings and 42 Elephants* and *Hungry Ants,* use children's books as contexts for thinking about division.

Sharing Candy Bars presents a division problem that engages students in thinking geometrically. In *Division Stories,* children write division word problems.

"A Suggested Daily Schedule" (see pages 9–11) includes a day-by-day plan for introducing and processing menu activities. It's helpful if the first menu tasks you introduce extend children's previous experiences. Familiar

tasks help children make the adjustment from whole class instruction to independent work.

An assortment of materials is used for the menu activities. Color Tiles and dice are needed for *Leftovers with Any Number.* Students need 1½-ounce boxes of raisins for *Raisins in the Big Box.* Paper rectangles divided into six squares each are the "candy bars" for *Sharing Candy Bars.*

Menu activities that require students to work in pairs are marked with a P in the upper right-hand corner, those that can be done individually are marked with an I, and those that require group work are marked with a G. Also, check page 4 for suggestions about organizing the menu activities and materials.

FROM THE CLASSROOM

Lynne explained to the children that before they began the menu they needed to set up their folders. She had made a construction-paper folder for each child, using two sheets of 12-by-18-inch paper. She folded one sheet "hot dog" style and the other "hamburger" style. She inserted the "hamburger" sheet into the "hot dog" sheet and taped them together so each folder had four pockets.

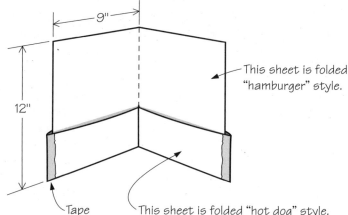

On the front of their folders the children wrote their names and *Math Menu: Division.* Then they opened their folders and wrote *Unfinished* on the left-hand pocket and *Finished* on the right-hand pocket. On the back pocket they wrote *Copy.*

"Remember," Lynne explained, "if you work with a partner and your partner needs a copy of the work for his or her folder, put it in the back pocket, and I'll know to make a copy. If you need more than one copy, write a message telling how many copies you need."

After the children wrote their names on their folders and on all their papers, they wrote their personal numbers next to their names. (These numbers corresponded to their alphabetical placement on the class list and made filing more efficient. When someone new joined the class, the children were anxious to know, "Does her last name come before or after mine in the alphabet?" They needed to know if their number would change. Lynne didn't change numbers, however, but assigned numbers for new students from the end of the class.)

As the children watched, Lynne wrote the contents of the menu on a chart:

Division Menu

1. The Doorbell Rings Again   I or P
2. Leftovers with Any Number   P

———— ———— ————

(lines are for names of different partners)

3. Raisins in the Big Box (1½ oz)   G

———— ———— ————

(may be done with up to three other students)

4. Candy Box Family Guides   I or P
5. 17 Kings and 42 Elephants   I or P
6. Sharing Candy Bars   P
7. Hungry Ants   I
8. Division Stories   I

"Remember," cautioned Lynne, "don't do a menu item until I've explained it, and I won't explain them all at once. I'll circle them as I introduce them, so you'll know which ones you can choose."

A Typical Menu Day

About halfway through the unit, Lynne called the students to the floor at the front of the room and asked for their attention so that she could help them get focused. "Several children have been absent the past few days," she began. "So let's go over the menu directions quickly. I want to be sure that everybody understands what the menu choices are so far. And I'm going to introduce one new menu item: *Sharing Candy Bars.*"

Lynne asked for volunteers to explain the five activities she had already introduced. For *The Doorbell Rings Again,* several children described the activity and offered things that could be shared when the doorbell rang. Lynne reminded the class of the data they had collected about family sizes before doing the *Candy Box Family Guides* menu activity.

Once the review was over, Lynne explained *Sharing Candy Bars,* and then the children got to work. They were eager to check their folders to see what they could do. Did they have something to finish from yesterday, or could they choose something new today? Several pairs—Irene and Matthew, Calie and Justine, and Patricia and Cynthia—chose the new task. Courtney, who loves to write, went back to work on *The Doorbell Rings Again.* Ethan agreed to work with Kent and Aaron on *Raisins in the Big Box.* Wesley, a quiet boy who seems to prefer working alone, told Lynne he didn't have a partner. Lynne sometimes gives shy children a nudge, but she doesn't create groups for them. She suggested, "Keith looks as if he's ready. Why don't you ask him?" Keith readily agreed to work with Wesley, and they decided to do *Leftovers with Any Number,* starting with 12 tiles. Tano and Kent also started a game of Leftovers. Lynne circulated for a while, then joined Tano and Kent to watch them play part of a game. Jamie and Shannon continued their game of Leftovers from yesterday, as did Gabrielle and Brenna.

Jamie and Shannon finished their game of
Leftovers with 25.

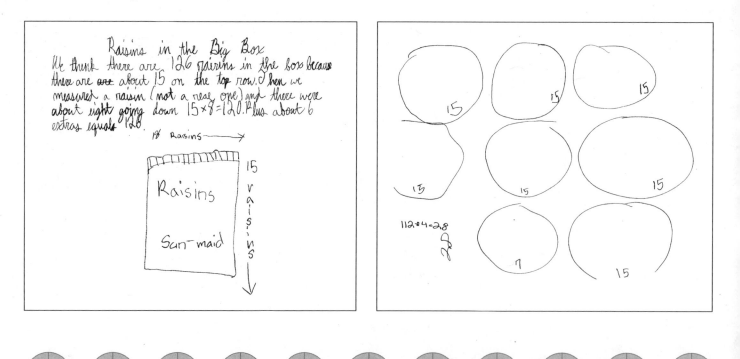

Leftovers with 25

$25 \div 4 = 6$ R①
$24 \div 3 = 8$ RO
$24 \div 2 = 12$ RO
$24 \div 6 = 4$ RO
$24 \div 6 = 4$ RO
$24 \div 3 = 8$ RO
$24 \div 4 = 6$ RO
$24 \div 2 = 12$ RO
$24 \div 5 = 4$ R④
$20 \div 4 = 5$ RO
$20 \div 6 = 3$ R②
$18 \div 5 = 3$ R③
$15 \div 6 = 2$ R③
$12 \div 2 = 6$ RO
$12 \div 2 = 6$ RO
$12 \div 6 = 2$ RO
$12 \div 5 = 2$ R②
$10 \div 2 = 5$ RO
$10 \div 1 = 10$ RO
$10 \div 6 = 1$ R④

$6 \div 4 = 1$ R②
$4 \div 2 = 2$ RO
$4 \div 5 = 0$ R④

	S	J
	8	1
	3	4
+	4	2
	—	+ 3
	7	2
		4
		—
		18

$$18 + 7 = 25$$

Wesley, Truc, Demetrius, and Kyle explained
how they estimated 126 raisins in the big box.
Then, when they grouped the raisins by 15s,
they found there were 112 in all, and that
each of them would get 28.

When Wesley and Keith finished *Leftovers with Any Number,* they showed their paper to Lynne and she checked their calculations. Wesley then joined Truc, Demetrius, and Kyle for *Raisins in the Big Box.* They estimated 126 raisins, but found there were 112. To share them, the boys used the calculator to divide 112 by 4.

Hugh had been wandering around the room trying to find a partner. He and Reggie had teamed up—temporarily. Hugh wanted to do the *Raisins in the Big Box,* but Reggie didn't. When they couldn't agree, Reggie joined Keith for *Sharing Candy Bars,* and Hugh continued wandering.

Reggie and Keith showed how to divide five candy bars among four people.

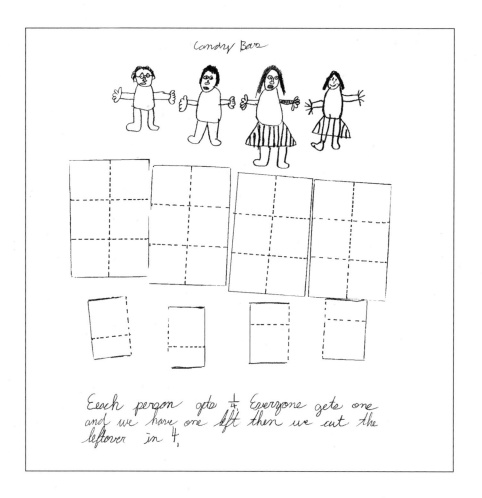

Lara and Vivian teamed up to work on the *Candy Box Family Guides.*

Samantha and Veronica also worked on the *Candy Box Family Guides* task. However, although they sat side by side, the two girls were making separate guides. Samantha was concentrating on making elaborate decorations for the cover and one inside page. It seemed as if she had chosen this project for the chance to draw with markers. But as so often happens in classrooms, appearances can be deceiving. When asked why she chose this particular topic, Samantha explained, "I just wanted to get it over with. I did not finish my multiplication menu, so this time I'm trying to get the big jobs done first. I picked this one because it looks like the biggest job to me."

Samantha then noticed that Amari was crying and asked her what was wrong. Amari had been working with Brittany on the *Candy Box Family Guides*. "I was doing it perfect and Brittany redid it," Amari responded. "It's a waste and she messed up my desk, and I just wish she'd never been born."

During the lunch break, Lynne talked to Brittany and Amari about the responsibility of working together. She gave them the option of working out their difficulties or starting over separately, making it clear that the responsibility was theirs.

At the end of the period that day, Lynne called the class together. "I noticed that Demetrius and Aaron worked well together today," she commented, and then asked the boys, "What do you think you did to make me think you were good partners?"

Aaron replied, "Demetrius helped me find the right answer."

"How did you decide who would go first?"

"It didn't matter to us," said Demetrius.

"Gabrielle, what made your work go well with Brenna? Did you have any disagreements? Did you both know what to do?" Through ongoing conversations about working relationships, Lynne helps children see how to work at being partners.

Lara and Vivian explained their recommendation for families of four.

> ### Families of Four
>
> Dear families of four,
> these are the ways we found
> for families of four. You can buy
> boxes so each person would get
> two candies and so each person
> would get one candy. Have a nice
> day.
>
> 4 X 2   4 X 1
>
>   4 X 1
>
>   4 X 2

MENU ACTIVITY

Overview

The Doorbell Rings Again

In the whole class lesson *The Doorbell Rang,* students learned what could happen when cookies had to be divided among a growing number of people. In this extension of that lesson, students use their understanding of division (with and without remainders) and develop their writing skills as they write their own stories. They may work on the activity individually or in pairs.

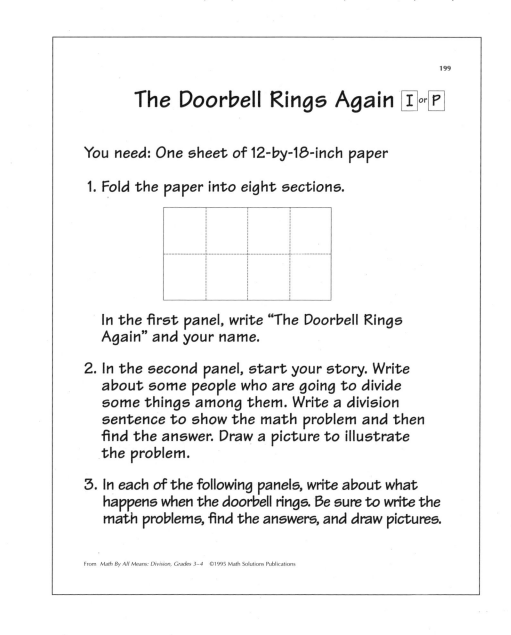

199

The Doorbell Rings Again I or P

You need: One sheet of 12-by-18-inch paper

1. Fold the paper into eight sections.

   In the first panel, write "The Doorbell Rings Again" and your name.

2. In the second panel, start your story. Write about some people who are going to divide some things among them. Write a division sentence to show the math problem and then find the answer. Draw a picture to illustrate the problem.

3. In each of the following panels, write about what happens when the doorbell rings. Be sure to write the math problems, find the answers, and draw pictures.

From *Math By All Means: Division, Grades 3–4*   ©1995 Math Solutions Publications

Before the lesson

Gather these materials:
■ *The Doorbell Rang* by Pat Hutchins (See Children's Books section on page 186.)
■ 12-by-18-inch paper, one per student or pair of students
■ Blackline master of menu activity, page 199

Getting started

■ Remind the students of the book *The Doorbell Rang.* If you feel it's necessary, read the book again and discuss what happens each time the doorbell rings.

■ Tell the students that they will work individually or in pairs to write their own stories about things that need to be shared. Talk with them about things that can be shared when the doorbell rings.

■ Explain that students are to follow the structure of *The Doorbell Rang* and either write their own stories about sharing cookies or create new stories with different items to share each time the doorbell rings.

■ Remind the children how to fold a 12-by-18-inch sheet of paper into eight sections, as they did in the whole class lesson *The Doorbell Rang.* Explain that, as before, students are to write in each panel what happens each time the doorbell rings.

FROM THE CLASSROOM

"For this menu activity," Lynne began, "you'll get to write your own version of *The Doorbell Rang."* The students seemed eager and interested.

"Who remembers what happened in the story?" Lynne asked. Almost half of the students raised their hands.

"Why don't you begin, Gabrielle?" Lynne said.

"There was a boy and a girl, and they were going to eat 12 cookies," Gabrielle said.

"Their names were Victoria and Sam," Courtney interrupted.

Gabrielle nodded her agreement. "But then the doorbell rang and two more kids came," Gabrielle continued, "so they had to share the cookies."

"Then what happened?" Lynne asked. "Who would like to tell what came next in the story?" She called on Kent.

"The doorbell rang again and more kids came," he said.

"How many more came?" Lynne asked.

"Two!" several students chorused.

"They had to share the cookies again," Irene added.

"And what happened next?" Lynne asked. She called on Reggie.

"Right before they could even take a bite, the doorbell rang, and six more kids came," he said. "So they were down to one cookie each."

Lynne called on Brittany, who said, "Then the doorbell rang again, but it was Grandma with a whole plate of cookies."

"It was in the nick of time," Ethan added.

Lynne explained the new activity. "For this menu task," Lynne said, "you'll write your own stories about things that can be shared and what happened when the doorbell rang. We'll call these stories 'The Doorbell Rings Again.' What sorts of things do you think could be shared?"

"Pizza," Matthew offered.

"Kittens," Courtney said, predictably.

"Could we use cookies?" Brenna asked.

"Yes," Lynne answered, "but you should make up a different story."

"Money, like we did before," Truc said recalling the *Sharing Money* whole class lesson.

"Candy," Ashley said.

Lynne then explained how the students were to present their stories. She folded a sheet of 12-by-18-inch paper into eight sections the way she had for the whole class lesson *The Doorbell Rang.* "Write the title, 'The Doorbell Rings Again,' in the first panel," Lynne said. "In the second panel, tell what is being shared and describe the people who are sharing it. Then, in each of the other panels, write about what happened when the doorbell rang."

"Do we draw pictures?" Patricia wanted to know.

"Yes," Lynne answered "You also need to write the math problem and its answer in each panel."

"Can we work together?" Justine asked.

"Yes," Lynne responded, "you can work with a partner or write your own story."

Observing the Children

While many children opted to use the same structure as the original story and write about sharing cookies, others wrote about sharing different things, most typically pizzas, but also money, muffins, and cupcakes. Some children used the names of others in their class, while some used those of family members. The children also brought their own brand of humor and silliness into their stories. For example, Jamie and Gabrielle's story began: *There were 2 kids and 15 cookies.* By the time the doorbell rang the second time with Irene, Ashley, Samantha, and Vivian appearing, Gabrielle wrote, *Oh my, do we have to share all the cookies with four more starving kids? Don't their moms ever feed them?* By the time the doorbell had rung two more times, with more children wanting to share cookies, she wrote: *Gabrielle was about to faint.* In the last episode, Gabrielle showed Mrs. Zolli saving the day by appearing at the door with 300 cookies and giving each of the 12 children an equal share of 25 cookies.

When Lynne asked the girls why the original 15 cookies didn't figure into the final equation, Gabrielle said, "Oh, the children had already eaten them."

Irene wrote about sharing pizza but used her experience from the *Dividing Cookies* whole class lesson. Her story focused on one large pizza and began: *Katy and her brother Jimmy were sitting down to a large pizza. When the doorbell rang.* Irene drew the pizza divided into two halves. Then Mom and Dad arrived, so she cut the pizza into fourths. Irene continued, dividing the pizza into sixths, eighths, and ninths. She ended her story: *By that time everybody had lost there apatite and they all went outside. The pizza got cold and they threw it out.*

Irene's story showed her understanding of fractions.

Demetrius also wrote a story about sharing pizza. He thought big, however, and his story began: *Kevin Had 200 pizzas when the doorbell rang.* He divided the pizzas among 2, 4, 8, and then 10 people.

Demetrius started his story with 200 pizzas, and ended it with zero pizzas.

Courtney's story also focused on pizza and, as does all her work, it starred kittens. When she showed Lynne her story, Lynne pointed out that after panel three, Courtney had become so interested in drawing cats and making up their conversations that she forgot the equations. Courtney went back to work.

Justine, who is devoted to the calculator, teamed up with Amari to write a doorbell story about Mom making more and more cupcakes for a party. The calculator provided equal shares of 1.6 and 1.2. The girls didn't "translate" these figures.

Patricia's story began with 21 cookies and herself. Other family members arrived—her "second" sister, older sister, father, mother, aunt, and uncle. Patricia showed how to share the 21 cookies each time.

Patricia's story focused on her family sharing 21 cookies.

Aaron is acknowledged by his peers as a gentle and cooperative boy and admired because he plays math games for the fun of it and not because he is eager to win. He paired up with Wesley, one of the quietest boys in the class, to write a story about fighting Hulk Hogan for cookies. They also battled another potential cookie eater, smashing his glasses (though the narrator immediately reported that Wesley paid for the damage). Although caught up in their exciting narrative, Wesley and Aaron didn't lose sight of the mathematics in their tale. As they were stuffing Hulk into a trash can (and later pulling him out), they made their story line fit these equations:

$$30 \div 2 = 15$$
$$30 \div 4 = 7\frac{1}{2}$$
$$30 \div 5 = 6$$
$$20 \div 5 = 4$$

Third-grade-boys' excitement with mayhem seemed to sweep through the room. Truc and Keith began their story with 100 low-fat cookies. The doorbell rang with *50 more cookies just for us.* Then Demetrius rang the doorbell and brought 100 more cookies. Truc and Keith threw a pie in his face, so they could have all the cookies: $250 \div 2 = 125$. The doorbell rang again and it was Hugh, bringing 100 more cookies. Truc and Keith ended their story with "mean Wesley" ringing the doorbell and eating all the cookies: $350 \div 1 = 350$. Thus, Keith brought into the story a problem that had amazed him during Leftovers: $15 \div 1 = 15$.

The students' choices revealed their level of comfort with numbers. Brenna, for example, wrote about sharing muffins, beginning with 6 muffins for one person, then two, three, and four people. When Grandma arrived, she brought 10 more muffins, and Brenna solved 16 divided by 4. She ended her story: *Then the doorbell rang again and again and again and again till it broke.*

A Class Discussion

Rather than leading one class discussion on the children's stories, Lynne had a few students share each day for several days. Then she compiled the stories into a large book, making a construction paper cover. The students enjoyed hearing one another's stories and went back to read them from time to time.

Kent's story began with $1,000,000.

MENU ACTIVITY

Overview

Leftovers with Any Number

Leftovers with Any Number extends children's experiences in the whole class lesson *The Game of Leftovers.* (See page 60.) Students play Leftovers again but with one difference: They choose how many Color Tiles to start with. This rule change gives students the opportunity to build their number sense about dividing numbers larger than 15. Also, students who decide to create their own die bring an element of strategy into a game of chance. A special message to teachers, "A Mathematical Note About Dividing by Zero," appears at the end of the lesson.

200

Leftovers with Any Number P

You Need: One die
 Color Tiles
 One cup to hold the tiles
 Six paper plates or 3-inch paper
 squares ("plates")

1. Choose how many tiles you want to start with.

2. Play a game of Leftovers.

3. When you finish the game, look at each of your sentences with a remainder of zero (RO). Write on the class chart each sentence with RO that isn't already posted.

From *Math By All Means: Division, Grades 3–4* ©1995 Math Solutions Publications

---

Before the lesson

Gather these materials for each pair of students:
■ One die
■ Six 3-by-3-inch squares of construction paper
■ 15–30 Color Tiles
■ One paper cup or other container to hold Color Tiles
■ Blank cubes and sticky labels for dice
■ Blackline master of menu activity, page 200

Getting started

■ If needed, review the directions for playing Leftovers.

■ Tell the children that for this menu task, they again play Leftovers, this time starting with any number of Color Tiles they choose. They should title their recording sheets "Leftovers with __," filling in the number of tiles they started with. Ask the children to think as they play about what number of tiles is a good strategy for the first player in a game. Also, tell them that they can use a regular die or one that they invent, as they did in the whole class lesson.

■ Instruct the students to play with at least three different partners and continue to record new division statements with remainders of zero on the class chart.

■ Use the following questions for a later class discussion:
How many Color Tiles did you use? Why?
What numbers did you put on the die you created? Why?
What discoveries did you make about dividing different numbers?

■ Have children examine their recording sheets and look for patterns in the remainders for various divisors. For example, divisors of 2 result in remainders of only zero or 1, divisors of 3 produce only remainders of 1 and 2, and so on. Point out that there can't be a remainder equal to or greater than a divisor or else there would be enough Color Tiles to put another on each "plate."

FROM THE CLASSROOM

Lynne's introduction to *Leftovers with Any Number* was brief. By this time, the students were comfortable with the game. Lynne described their options for this activity. "This time you can start with any number of tiles you want," she said. "Also, you can use a regular die or one you created."

"Can we make another die if we want?" Irene asked.

"Yes," Lynne responded.

"I mean a different one than we already made," Irene wanted to be sure.

"That would be fine," Lynne answered.

"What if we start with only two tiles?" Carey wanted to know, testing Lynne's limits.

"Would you rather go first or second?" Lynne asked.

"First!" Carey answered. "Definitely first."

"I don't think it would be much fun," Truc added. "It would be over in a minute."

Lynne gave one more instruction. "Keep adding sentences with remainders of zero to the class chart," she reminded them.

The students were interested in trying Leftovers with other numbers. They were familiar with the game and curious about how different numbers would affect it.

Observing the Children

Brenna and Irene played Leftovers with 8, using a regular die. Later, Brenna changed partners and played with Gabrielle, saying, "Leftovers with 8 didn't last very long. Let's try 15." But that game had one less move than Leftovers with 8, so Brenna concluded that "the number you start with doesn't decide the length of the game."

Keith and Demetrius chose to play Leftovers with 12, and their game resulted in a tie.

Keith and Demetrius's game ended in a tie.

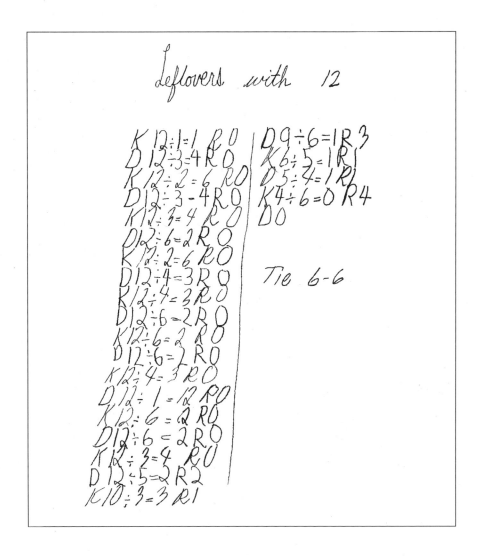

Robin and Ashley played Leftovers with a regular die. They started with 28 tiles. Robin rolled a 5, put out five plates, and divided the tiles. Both girls recorded: *28 ÷ 5 = 5 R3*. They took away the 3 leftovers and then counted the remaining tiles to get 25. Each time they had leftovers, they counted the tiles to see how many were left for the next round.

Matthew wanted to start with 24 tiles because, "You can divide it fast."

"What do you mean?" Lynne asked him.

"It's an easy number" he replied.

Calie and Justine had started with 20 tiles and were on their third turn when Lynne noticed that the equation they had just written was wrong: $15 \div 6 = 2 R1$.

"Show me how you figured that," Lynne said.

Calie started counting out the 15 tiles onto the six plates.

Justine said, "2 remainder 3." Then she gasped, "OOH," noticing the answer written on her paper. The girls began to fix their papers.

Justine was eager to throw the die. "I got 6," she announced, while Calie was still trying to change the remainder from the previous round.

"Wait!" protested Calie.

Justine kept going. Lynne interceded. "Wait. What has to happen before Justine rolls the dice?"

"I take my leftovers," said Calie.

"Oh, sorry," Justine said. Lynne reminded them not to rush.

Aaron and Ethan had also started with 20 tiles. Now 12 tiles were left, and they had each rolled three times without getting any remainders. A crowd of children had gathered around to see what was happening. Lynne joined them.

"We're stuck," Aaron grinned. "We've rolled three times each."

Lynne asked them, "What could you roll that would give you leftovers?" They both thought a while. Aaron said, "A 5."

"Only a 5?" asked Lynne.

Aaron thought again and then nodded.

"This could take a while," Ethan rolled his eyes.

"Maybe we should make a different die," Aaron said. The other children dispersed, and Lynne continued circulating.

Aaron and Ethan rolled eight times before getting past the number 12.

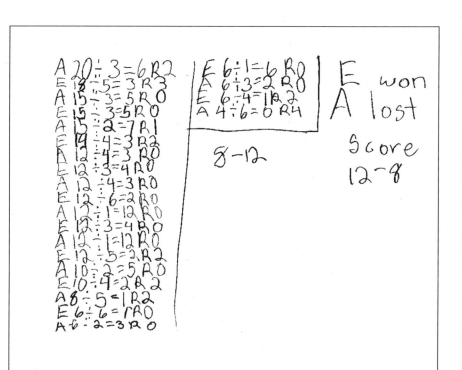

Keith and Demetrius came up to Lynne. Demetrius exclaimed, "We had a tie!"

"Yeah," Keith added, "you shouldn't start with an even number!"

"Why do you say that?" Lynne asked.

"If you pick an even number, you might end up in a tie," explained Demetrius. "That won't happen with an odd number. With an odd number, someone has to win."

"Let's talk about that in a class discussion," Lynne said. "Then we can see what others think. Why don't you try some more games to test your theory?" The boys nodded and raced back to their seats.

Lynne noticed that in several of the students' games, they had made mistakes part way through. In these cases, she had them go back and play from the error.

Vivian and Jasmine played Leftovers with 25. "We got stuck on a lot of numbers," said Valerie.

"Which ones?" asked Lynne.

Vivian looked at her sheet. "Mostly 12 and 18," she replied.

A Class Discussion

At the end of the first class period after she had introduced *Leftovers with Any Number*, Lynne called the students to the front of the room and began a class discussion. She wanted everyone in the class to hear Demetrius and Keith's theory about starting with even numbers. Whenever possible, Lynne likes to incorporate students' experiences and observations into class discussions. That way, students see how their thinking can contribute to the class learning. Also, Lynne was interested in how the others would respond to the boys' conjecture.

"Demetrius and Keith," Lynne said, "how about sharing your idea about playing Leftovers?"

"Don't start with an even number!" the boys said emphatically, and then laughed because they had said it in unison.

"It always ends in a tie," Keith explained.

"We did two games—with 12 tiles and then with 16, and it was a tie both times," Demetrius added.

"Really? Is that true?" asked Aaron.

"It's true," Irene chimed in. "Brenna and I started with 10 and we ended in a tie. And 10's an even number."

"But Ethan and I played with 10, and he ended up with 7 leftovers when I only had 3. That wasn't a tie," protested Aaron.

Kent offered, "When Wesley and I started with 10, we didn't end up in a tie either. He won."

"Well, I'm picking an odd number when I play again," insisted Keith.

"Me, too!" exclaimed Reggie. He had not yet chosen Leftovers on the menu, but like most children he kept "tuned in" to what was happening in other corners of the room and was aware of what his classmates were doing.

"This is certainly something that would be interesting to investigate," Lynne stated. "As you play Leftovers with Any Number, watch out for tie games. Aaron and Kent have pointed out that games that start with an even number of tiles don't always end in a tie. But you can watch out to see if they often do. You can also watch out to see if you ever play a game starting with an odd number of tiles that ends in a tie."

NOTE It usually makes sense to wait until everyone has had a chance to do a menu activity before initiating a class discussion. However, at times, it is appropriate to discuss an activity after only some of the students have chosen it. Others can benefit from their experiences or suggest ideas that other students might consider.

NOTE Teachers sometimes need to decide when to resolve mathematical issues for children and when to leave issues unsolved. It's important to resist giving solutions just to bring closure to a discussion. Many mathematical problems are not easily or quickly solved, and we want to help children develop the kind of persistence that mathematical thinking often demands.

Kent and Wesley started their game with 10 tiles.

Leftovers

W 10 ÷ 5 = 2 R 0

K 10 ÷ 1 = 10 R 0

W 10 ÷ 2 = 5 R 0

K 10 ÷ 2 = 5 R 0

W 10 ÷ 4 = 2 R 2

K 8 ÷ 1 = 8 R 0

W 8 ÷ 6 = 1 R 2

K 6 ÷ 2 = 3 R 0

W 6 ÷ 3 = 2 R 0

K 6 ÷ 5 = 1 R 1

W 5 ÷ 6 = 0 R 5

A Later Class Discussion

After all the children had had a chance to play the game, Lynne asked them to bring their *Leftovers with Any Number* recording sheets to the front of the room for another discussion.

"Who has a number that's good for starting a game?" Lynne said to begin the conversation. "One where the first player gets something for sure."

"I think 17," said Calie.

"Let's see," answered Lynne. "Let's try all the numbers on a die with 17." She asked the children to supply answers to the division problems as she wrote them on the board. She did not encourage speedy replies but was careful to give the children time to think. Also, Lynne recorded two ways, showing the children how subtracting was useful to figuring out the remainders.

$$17 \div 1 = 17 \qquad 17 \div 2 = 8\ R1 \qquad 17 \div 3 = 5\ R2$$

$$1\overline{)17} \quad \begin{array}{r} 17 \\ \underline{17} \\ 0 \end{array} \qquad\qquad 2\overline{)17} \quad \begin{array}{r} 8\ R1 \\ \underline{16} \\ 1 \end{array} \qquad\qquad 3\overline{)17} \quad \begin{array}{r} 5\ R2 \\ \underline{15} \\ 2 \end{array}$$

$$17 \div 4 = 4\ R1 \qquad 17 \div 5 = 3\ R2 \qquad 17 \div 6 = 2\ R5$$

$$4\overline{)17} \quad \begin{array}{r} 4\ R1 \\ \underline{16} \\ 1 \end{array} \qquad\qquad 5\overline{)17} \quad \begin{array}{r} 3 \\ \underline{15} \\ 2 \end{array} \qquad\qquad 6\overline{)17} \quad \begin{array}{r} 2\ R5 \\ \underline{12} \\ 5 \end{array}$$

"What do you think?" asked Lynne. "Remember when we played before and talked about how hard it was to get off 12? Would you rather start with 12 or 17?"

NOTE Using correct terminology, such as factor and divisor, in the context of a familiar game helps students become familiar with mathematical language. Students need repeated experiences with terminology to learn the meaning of the words and begin to use them.

"I'd say 17," said Courtney. "Every time you roll the die, you get a leftover, except with 1."

"Seventeen is a good number for a game," agreed Truc.

"You can really get stuck on 12," Aaron added.

"Also, you can't end up in a tie because 17 doesn't split into two numbers evenly," Demetrius said, referring to his earlier discovery.

"Look at your lists," Lynne said. "Are there any other numbers that you get stuck on easily?"

Several children called out responses. "6." "10." "24." "6."

"These numbers have more factors than others," Lynne said. "They have more numbers that go into them evenly, more divisors that give a remainder of zero."

"Nothing goes into 13," Matthew observed.

"You forgot 1," Irene countered.

"Yeah, well, 1 goes into everything," Matthew said.

"That's because 1 is a factor of every number," Lynne added.

Lynne then asked the children to look at the remainders for different divisors. "Look at sentences where you divided the tiles on two plates, where you divided by 2," she said. "What do you notice about the remainders?" The children scanned their papers.

"They're all 1s!" Ashley said.

"Or zeros," Truc added.

"Why do you think there aren't any remainders greater than 1 when you share tiles on two plates?" Lynne probed. The children were quiet. All of a sudden, Aaron's hand shot up.

"Then you could share them," he said excitedly. The others didn't understand what he meant.

"Look," he said, "if you had like a remainder of 3, then you could put out 2 more tiles." Several students understood his thinking. Others were still confused.

"You can't have more than 1 left over," Aaron continued. "Then you would have more to share."

Not all of the children grasped Aaron's logic, but Lynne moved on. "Look at sentences where you divided by 3," she said. "What remainders did you get?"

"All 1s again," Brenna said. "Oh, no, there's a 2."

"It's 1s, 2s, and 0s," Courtney said.

Lynne started a chart on the board:

Divisor	Possible Remainders
2	0, 1
3	0, 1, 2

"What about for 4, 5, 6, and 1?" she asked. "Look over your sheets and talk to your neighbor." After a moment, she called them to attention.

"There's a pattern," Wesley said.

Lynne had the children report their findings. Finally the chart looked like this:

Divisor	Possible Remainders
1	0
2	0, 1
3	0, 1, 2
4	0, 1, 2, 3
5	0, 1, 2, 3, 4
6	0, 1, 2, 3, 4, 5

"That's neat!" Aaron said.

"So it's better to have big numbers on the die," Irene said. "You get more leftovers that way."

Lynne didn't feel it was necessary to explain the rationale for the remainders being at least one less than the divisors. Rather, she felt that this beginning experience would be useful later when they studied more about division.

Samantha and Juliette were surprised at how many times they rolled before getting a remainder for 20.

> **Leftovers with 20**
>
> $20 \div 4 = 5$ R0
> $20 \div 5 = 4$ RO
> $20 \div 1 = 20$ RO
> $20 \div 1 = 20$ RO
> $20 \div 2 = 10$ RO
> $20 \div 1 = 20$ RO
> $20 \div 2 = 10$ RO
> $20 \div 5 = 4$ RO
> $20 \div 2 = 10$ RO
> $20 \div 5 = 4$ RO
> $20 \div 1 = 20$ RO
> $20 \div 6 = 3$ (R2)
> $18 \div 3 = 6$ RO
> $18 \div 3 = 6$ RO
> $18 \div 6 = 3$ RO
> $18 \div 4 = 4$ (R2)
> $16 \div 2 = 8$ RO
> $16 \div 3 = 5$ (R1)
> $15 \div 2 = 7$ (R1)
>
> $14 \div 6 = 1$ (R5)
> $11 \div 4 = 4$ (R2)
> $4 \div 1 = 4$ RO
> $4 \div 1 = 4$ RO
> $4 \div 6 = 0$ R4
>
> $\begin{array}{r} +2 \\ +2 \\ +1 \\ +5 \\ +4 \\ \hline 14 \end{array}$ $\begin{array}{r} 1 \\ +2 \\ +1 \\ +2 \\ \hline 6 \end{array}$
>
> J   S
> 14 6

A Mathematical Note About Dividing by Zero

When the students were discussing what numbers to put on the dice they were making to play Leftovers, Matthew suggested that zero would be a good number. "If you get zero, all the tiles are leftovers, so you would win," he stated. A buzz of excitement went through the room.

Of course, Matthew wasn't correct. However, the issue of dividing by zero is complicated for children to understand. There are several ways to think about what happens when you divide a number by zero. For example, think about a simple division statement, such as $12 \div 3 = 4$. Because division is the inverse of multiplication, we can multiply to verify the answer: $4 \times 3 = 12$. If you multiply the answer to the division problem (the quotient) by the divisor, you should get the number you started with (the dividend). Here are some examples:

$$12 \div 12 = 1 \qquad 1 \times 12 = 12$$
$$12 \div 6 = 2 \qquad 2 \times 6 = 12$$
$$12 \div 4 = 3 \qquad 3 \times 4 = 12$$
$$12 \div 3 = 4 \qquad 4 \times 3 = 12$$
$$12 \div 2 = 6 \qquad 6 \times 2 = 12$$
$$12 \div 1 = 12 \qquad 12 \times 1 = 12$$

Now suppose you were trying to solve $12 \div 0$. Typically, children think the answer should be zero, but it doesn't check!

$$12 \div 0 = 0 \qquad 0 \times 0 = 0$$

Actually, no matter what answer you get, if you try to check it by multiplying, you run into difficulty because zero times any other number gives zero. Nothing will work. Here are some examples:

$$12 \div 0 = 1 \qquad 1 \times 0 = 0 \qquad \text{No}$$
$$12 \div 0 = 2 \qquad 2 \times 0 = 0 \qquad \text{No}$$
$$12 \div 0 = 3 \qquad 3 \times 0 = 0 \qquad \text{No}$$
$$12 \div 0 = 4 \qquad 4 \times 0 = 0 \qquad \text{No}$$
$$12 \div 0 = 6 \qquad 6 \times 0 = 0 \qquad \text{No}$$
$$12 \div 0 = 12 \qquad 12 \times 0 = 0 \qquad \text{No}$$

Here's another way to try to understand the difficulty of dividing by zero. In the examples showing 12 divided by different numbers listed in the first set of problems, 12 was divided by a smaller number each time, and the resulting answers got larger. This makes sense because dividing a number into fewer parts will produce more in each part. Continuing the pattern of dividing 12 by smaller and smaller numbers requires thinking about fractional divisors. Still, the pattern of increasing answers continues:

$$12 \div 12 = 1$$
$$12 \div 6 = 2$$
$$12 \div 4 = 3$$
$$12 \div 3 = 4$$
$$12 \div 2 = 6$$
$$12 \div 1 = 12$$
$$12 \div \tfrac{1}{2} = 24$$
$$12 \div \tfrac{1}{3} = 36$$
$$12 \div \tfrac{1}{4} = 48$$
$$12 \div \tfrac{1}{6} = 72$$
$$12 \div \tfrac{1}{12} = 144$$
$$12 \div \tfrac{1}{100} = 1200$$
$$12 \div \tfrac{1}{1000} = 12,000$$
$$12 \div \tfrac{1}{1,000,000} = 12,000,000$$

Dividing by $\frac{1}{1,000,000}$ is an example of dividing by a very small divisor. Not as small as zero, of course, but going in the direction of zero. A mathematician looking at the list of those division examples would notice several patterns and make several statements:

1. The dividend stays constant; it is always 12.
2. The divisors get smaller and smaller, getting closer and closer to zero.
3. The closer the divisor gets to zero, the larger the answer gets.
4. If the divisor reached zero, the answer would be enormous.

This leads to the conclusion that as the divisor approached zero, the answer approaches infinity. This discovery isn't particularly helpful or useful, however, when we're looking for a numerical answer to a division problem. So, what mathematicians have agreed upon is to say that "division by zero is undefined." Which means, the division has no answer that makes any sense, so we can't do it.

Investigating $0 \div 0$, however, seems interesting. Just as no number works for an answer to $12 \div 0$ (or any number divided by zero), it seems that it's possible to solve $0 \div 0$ and check it:

$$0 \div 0 \qquad\qquad 0 \times 0 = 0$$

However, that system of checking division by multiplying makes *any* answer to $0 \div 0$ correct!

$0 \div 0 = 0$	$0 \times 0 = 0$
$0 \div 0 = 1$	$1 \times 0 = 0$
$0 \div 0 = 2$	$2 \times 0 = 0$
$0 \div 0 = 50$	$50 \times 0 = 0$
$0 \div 0 = 600$	$600 \times 0 = 0$
$0 \div 0 = 1,000$	$1,000 \times 0 = 0$

Having any answer work is as problematic as having no answer work.

So you just can't divide by zero.

Explaining this to elementary school children can be tough. Some students may be fascinated by this sort of thinking; some will be confused; others will be completely disinterested. If you decide to offer an explanation, be sure to do so with a light touch, quit if students' eyes seem to glaze, and offer to continue with only those who are interested.

To return to the extension for Leftovers: Limiting children to the numbers 1 through 6 for their dice, as suggested in the whole class lesson, avoids the situation of explaining why it's not possible to divide by zero.

ASSESSMENT What Is 20 ÷ 4?

FROM THE CLASSROOM

This assessment checks whether students can interpret the symbolism of division and explain how to find an answer to a division problem. Introduce the assignment by writing on the board: *What is 20 ÷ 4?* Tell the children that you'd like them to describe each part of the mathematical symbolism, then explain the problem and how someone could find the answer. Tell them that they can use pictures or diagrams to illustrate their explanations. It may help some children to have the directions written on the board:

1. What does each part of 20 ÷ 4 mean?
2. How would you explain 20 ÷ 4 to someone who doesn't know about division?

Lynne introduced the assignment by asking the children to do a quick-write. She explained, "For a quick-write, you don't need to write a lot." She then wrote on the board:

What is 20 ÷ 4?

"That's easy," Aaron said.
"It's 5," Irene said.
Lynne prodded the children to think more about the problem. "This problem might be easy for some people," she said, "but I'm interested in knowing more than just the answer. I'd like you to explain each part of what I wrote on the board and explain how to find the answer. You might want to use pictures or diagrams."
"Can we use words?" Courtney wanted to know.
"Yes."
"Can we use an equal sign and a 5?" asked Keith.
"Yes."
Lynne then wrote on the board:

1. What does each part of 20 ÷ 4 mean?
2. How would you explain 20 ÷ 4 to someone who doesn't know about division?

"Are there any questions?" Lynne asked. There weren't. Lynne said, "When you're finished, you may work on the menu."
The children began to write, and most got busy immediately. As usual, a few had difficulty settling down. Hugh went over to sharpen his pencil, then sat down, then got up to sharpen his pencil again. He glanced at Lynne as he returned to his seat the second time, and she caught his eye. That seemed to be enough for Hugh to realize it was time to get to work.
Brenna, Brittany, and Amari were chatting, and Lynne wasn't sure what they were talking about. She wandered over and overheard Brittany say,

"But it doesn't always come out even. I know what I'm going to write." The three girls began writing.

When Keith went to get a calculator, Wesley said, "I don't need a calculator to do this one. It's easy." Keith shrugged.

Lynne thought that describing the assignment as a quick-write helps relax children who feel uneasy if they have to write a lot. "Also, we'd been talking regularly about the symbolism of division," Lynne commented, "and the children felt comfortable with explaining it. This was a good check that we were making progress."

Some children wrote explanations about each part of the equation. Matthew, for example, wrote: *20 means the object or thing your dividing. ÷ is a sign that tells us to divide. 4 means how many times your dividing the object. 5 is the answer that shows how you divided.* Matthew then illustrated with tally marks, making four groups of five tally marks each.

Brittany pointed out that division doesn't always come out even. She wrote: *The 20 means how mean* [many] *of some thing. The 4 means who is sharing it. This sign ÷ means divding eqley but some times it dus not come out eqley.* She included two illustrations that showed how to find the answer.

Kent wrote: *20 is the thing you divide with. ÷ means the subject that you divide with. 4 is the thing that you are dividing with. 5 is the answer to the question.*

(left) Matthew explained each part of the equation.

(right) Brittany pointed out that division doesn't always come out equally.

$20 \div 4 = ?$

20 means the object or thing your dividing.

÷ is a sign that tells us to divide.

4 means how many times your dividing the object.

5 is the answer that shows how you divided.

They both mean groups

What is $20 \div 4 = $ 5

The 20 means how mean of some thing.

The 4 means who is sharing it.

This sign ÷ means divding egley but some times it dus not come out egley.

$20 \div 4 = 5$

Ashley wrote: *The 20 mean what you divide. The four mean how you are going to divide them up. And the 5 means the answer.* She then relied on an illustration to explain how she would find the answer.

Other children described the meaning by referring to some context. Samantha, for example, wrote about sharing books: *The 20 means the number you pick to ÷ with. The ÷ sign means to make it equal, for exampal if you took 20 books and 4 people, then you would figuar out how each person gets five books.*

Ashley illustrated how she would find the answer to 20 ÷ 4.

*What is 20 ÷ 4?
The 20 mean what you divicle. The four mean how you are going to divide them up. And the 5 means the answer.*

How would I eiglen this problem.

Samantha understood the need for equal groups when dividing.

What is 20÷4?

The 20 means the number you pick to ÷ with. The ÷ sign means to make it equal, for exampal if you took 20 books and 4 people, thin you would figuar out how each person gets five books. Well, 4×5=20 and 5×4=20 and 20÷4=5 and 20÷5=4 and 5÷4= IR1 and 4÷5=0, nothing, you can't do it.

Demetrius wrote about pizzas: *20 ÷ 4 is 5. The 20 means what you are dividing. The 4 means how many people there are. The ÷ division sign tells you that you have to divide. And the 5 is how many things each person gets. Let's say there were 20 pizzas and 4 people. If each person were to get the same amount of pizza. How many pizza's would each person get?*

Justine referred to sharing cookies. She wrote: *Twenty is how many cookies to share with divideing sighn ÷ is to tell you what to do like + − × the five is the answer to the problem. The four is how many people. I would explain divition with a picture like this.*

Garrett, who has difficulty with most assignments, worked hard on this one. He wrote: *20 ÷ 4 is 5. the divion sign is dviding the numbers.*

What is 20÷4?

20÷4 is 5. The 20 means what you are dividing. The 4 means how many people there are. The ÷ division sigh tells you that you have to divide And the 5 is how many things each person gets. Let's say there were 20 pizza's and 4 people. If each person were to get the same amount of pizza. How many pizzas would each person get? 20÷4 sort of like multiplication because you need times to know 5x4 to figure out the problem,

---

What is 20÷4?

① Twenty is how many cookies to share with divideing sighn ÷ is to tell you what to do like + − × the five is the answer to the problem. The four is how many people. ② I would explain divition with a picture like this

20÷4=5

Person #1
Person #2
Person #3
Person #4

What is 20÷4?
20÷4 is 5 the divion sign is dviding the numbers.

(above left) Demetrius used sharing pizzas to explain 20 ÷ 4.

(above right) Justine used sharing cookies to explain 20 ÷ 4.

(below right) Garrett's response showed progress for him.

MENU ACTIVITY

Overview

Raisins in the Big Box

This extension of the whole class lesson *Explorations with Raisins* (see page 72) uses a larger box of raisins. In this activity, children work in groups of three or four to estimate, count, and share the raisins in a $1\frac{1}{2}$-ounce box. Sharing the raisins gives children additional experiences with dividing equally, and comparing the larger box to the $\frac{1}{2}$-ounce box gives them a chance to think proportionally.

201

Raisins in the Big Box ⬚G

You need: One $1\frac{1}{2}$-ounce box of raisins

1. Without opening the box, estimate how many raisins are inside. Write your estimate on a sheet of paper.

2. Empty the raisins onto a sheet of paper. Count them. Next to your estimate, write the total number of raisins and explain how you counted them.

3. Divide the raisins among the members of your group. Record how many raisins each person received and explain how you divided them.

From *Math By All Means: Division, Grades 3–4* ©1995 Math Solutions Publications

Before the lesson

Gather these materials:
■ 1¹/₂-ounce boxes of raisins, enough for one-third of the class
■ Blackline master of menu activity, page 201

Getting started

■ Remind students of the procedures they followed in the whole class lesson: Each student estimated how many raisins were in the box, counted the actual number of raisins, and shared the total number of raisins with everyone in the group.

■ Introduce the menu activity by explaining that students will work in groups of three or four. Each group will have one box. The students will estimate, count, and then share the raisins in that box.

■ Tell the students that their group should write one paper to report the number of raisins in the box and figure out how many each child got. Tell them they can eat the raisins when they are finished, but ask them to save the boxes so they can refer to them later.

FROM THE CLASSROOM

Lynne gathered the class at the front of the room to introduce *Raisins in the Big Box*. "It's like the whole class lesson we did," she explained, "but you'll use this larger box."

"Can we eat the raisins?" Carey wanted to know.

"After you've completed the task, you can eat them," Lynne responded.

She then referred to the earlier lesson. "Who remembers what we did first with the small boxes of raisins?" she asked. Hands went up. She called on Calie.

"We opened up the top and counted and guessed," she said.

"No," Justine corrected, "we just guessed first. Then we opened the box."

"Oh, yeah," Calie agreed.

"This time, you make just one guess," Lynne said. "Do it with the top closed. Here's a hint: Use the information we have about how many raisins were in the smaller boxes." She pointed to the chart of the results from the previous raisin activity.

"Then what did you do?" Lynne asked.

"We counted them," Ethan answered.

"We had to group them," Samantha added.

"Then we shared them," Brittany said, "and ate them."

"That's exactly what you'll do this time," Lynne said. "Estimate, count, and then divide them. You need to work in a group of three or four, and the number of people will determine how to share them. Also, your group should write just one paper to report what you found and how you did it. Any questions?"

There were none, and Lynne had one more direction. "When you're finished, don't throw the box away. Save it so we can refer to it later."

Observing the Children

Aaron, Kent, and Ethan, three mathematically able students, were eager to form a group. They guessed that the big box had 90 raisins, and recorded this number. When Lynne asked them why they guessed 90, Aaron explained.

"It's a 1¹/₂-ounce box," he said. "That's three times as big as the little box, and those little boxes had around 30 raisins, well more, but I think 90."

After making their estimate, the boys dumped the raisins on a sheet of paper in the center of their table. Each boy took a handful, and they arranged the raisins in groups of 20. They were surprised that only 81 raisins were in the box.

"These must be big raisins," concluded Ethan.

After a false start, the boys figured out that each person could have a group of 20, leaving 21, which they divided so each got 7 more. They concluded with a humorous note: *Now we can eat.*

Aaron, Kent, and Ethan divided 81 raisins among the three of them.

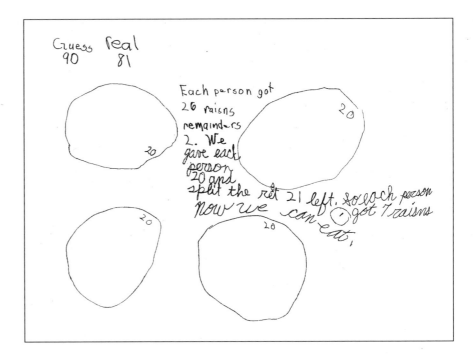

As soon as Lynne instructed the children to get to work on the menu, Hugh was left out. Everyone at his table wanted to be free of Hugh's peskiness and so quickly teamed up with someone else on a project—before Lynne even officially announced it was time for menu choices. Other children, wise to Hugh, also excluded him. Hugh wandered the room looking for a partner. Reggie, who cheerfully works with anybody at any time, was willing to be Hugh's partner, but Reggie wanted to do *Candy Box Family Guides*, and Hugh was determined to do *Raisins in the Big Box*. He started wandering again.

At this time, Garrett returned from his pullout program and decided he'd like to work on *Raisins in the Big Box*. He and Hugh seemed to realize they would not make a good team and carefully avoided each other. Finally, Hugh gave up and sat by himself, tracing his name on his math folder. Lynne sat and talked with him about choosing an activity.

"I don't want to work alone," he said.

"I noticed that Reggie was interested in being your partner," Lynne responded.

"But he wouldn't do the *Raisins in the Big Box* one," Hugh answered.

"Well, then it seems you'll have to choose one to do alone," Lynne said.

"Can I do the raisins one by myself?" Hugh asked.

Lynne paused. This is one of those situations that demands a response, and there's no easy choice. Lynne realizes that she can't solve Hugh's social problem, but she doesn't want him to be isolated. It's hard to know when to cater to a child and when to stick to classroom demands. She suggested a compromise. "How about today you do something by yourself," she said. "Then, tomorrow, when Grandpa is here, perhaps you can do *Raisins in the Big Box* with him. (Grandpa is a volunteer who visits Lynne's classroom regularly and enjoys helping the children with math.) Hugh agreed.

Demetrius, Truc, Kyle, and Wesley chose to work together. They estimated 62, then grouped the raisins by 10s.

"We were way off," Truc commented when they found they had a total of 86 raisins.

They used a calculator to divide their total, explaining that they knew .5 meant $\frac{1}{2}$. The "4 copies" on the boys' recording sheet indicated that they were following the class procedure for letting Lynne know to make four photocopies, one for each of their folders.

Demetrius, Kyle, Truc, and Wesley explained their understanding that .5 is the same as $\frac{1}{2}$.

> *Raisins In The Big Box*
>
> Estimate: 62   Real: 86
>
> We counted by 10's and 6 leftover. So we added 6 to 80 and we got 86. To divide them, we put 86÷4 in the calculator and we got 21.5 and we know that .5 means a $\frac{1}{2}$.

Garrett carried two boxes of raisins over to Carey and asked him if he wanted to do raisin research. Carey responded, "Sure!" and told Garrett to put one of the boxes back, explaining that they needed only one box. "It's a big box," he said, "and we share it."

Garrett estimated that there were 99 raisins in the box; Carey predicted 64.

"And you can't change your guess!" announced Carey as they dumped the raisins out of the box and started grouping them by 5s, drawing a circle around each group. Lynne noticed the two boys working together. Even though they weren't working in a group of three or four, she let them continue, pleased that they were engaged. Garrett often has difficulty working effectively.

Carey counted 95 raisins altogether. Garrett tried to confirm, counting by 5s, but he got stuck at 40.

Carey suggested, "As I take them away, you write 5 in the circle." They discovered they hadn't grouped their raisins accurately; some circles had 4, others 7. They fixed the groups, counted together, and recorded their new count of 97.

Lynne asked them, "If you split the raisins equally, how many would each of you get?"

"I get 97; Garrett doesn't want any," announced Carey.

"But what if you did split them evenly, how many would you get?" Lynne persisted.

Carey thought a moment and then said, "Somewhere around 40-something." Lynne noted that Carey, although he has learning difficulties, particularly in reading and writing, does have a real-world number sense, something that Garrett lacks. Lynne also noted that, for the moment, dividing things in half is challenge enough for Carey and Garrett.

Meanwhile, Hugh had resumed his efforts to find a group to do *Raisins in the Big Box*. He noticed Shannon and Veronica just completing their work. He asked Shannon to do it again, this time with him. "We can do it—just us two—but we can pretend there are three." Shannon looked doubtful but then agreed. Hugh went to get a box of raisins.

When he returned, he started to open the box. Shannon reminded him, "We have to guess first." She took the box and closed the top. Hugh guessed 50; Shannon guessed 30.

Hugh opened the box and saw eight raisins on top. He looked at the side of the box and said, "It looks like eight rows . . . and 8 plus 8 is 16 plus 8 is 24 plus 8 is 32 . . . I'll change my guess to 32."

Hugh and Shannon dumped the raisins out of the box and started grouping them by 5s. After counting by 5s, Hugh thought they had 82 in all. Shannon, who is never without a calculator in math class, punched in numbers and thought they had 86, but Hugh convinced her they had 82.

"Now we have to divide them," said Hugh. Shannon started counting one by one.

"It's 41," said Hugh, "because 41 plus 41 equals 82."

"How many each would four people get?" asked Lynne to push the children's mathematical understanding. Neither Hugh nor Shannon seemed willing to tackle this problem.

Hugh insisted they had to write up what they did. "Before we forget it," he said. He started writing. He didn't know how to spell *raisins,* but Shannon found the box and spelled it for him. She also dictated a sentence: *We got 82 raisins in the big box.* Shannon was amazed to see on the calculator that 82 divided by 2 was 41. The calculator answer was more real for her than any paper-and-pencil answer could ever be. Hugh said, "I knew it in my head," and was not interested in the calculator solution.

"What did you learn?" Lynne asked Hugh and Shannon.

"Raisins are very good," smiled Hugh as he ate. He and Shannon sat quietly eating raisins and talking.

Shannon seemed to enjoy this activity so much that she repeated it three days later, this time with Justine, Jamie, and Gabrielle. When asked to estimate how many raisins were in the box, Gabrielle guessed 26, Justine 42, and Jamie 43. Shannon picked 40, apparently not seeing any connection between that box and the fact that 82 raisins were in the box she had examined with Hugh. This team grouped their raisins by 10s and then divided raisins 20 at a time.

NOTE It's always difficult when a teacher realizes that what she is teaching is out of reach and inappropriate for a particular child. A teacher must always consider a student's self-esteem as well as his or her intellectual success; the two are, of course, intertwined.

Hugh and Shannon divided 82 raisins between them.

We did it by fives.
We got 82 raisins in the big box.
We both got 41 each.
We passout one at a teim.

The rules for menu work include: Complete each item on the menu and don't work with the same person on two activities in a row. But a teacher must know when to bend the rules. Shannon and Garrett both operate on the fringes of this class. If Garrett and Carey can successfully team up for two activities in a row, and if Shannon can be a contributing partner in two different raisin research teams, then Lynne feels the regular rules need not apply.

When Reggie, Matthew, and Calie teamed up, their box had 81 raisins in it. They divided the raisins accurately. First, they each got 20, then 6 more, and finally 1. Their drawing was correct, although including "R1" was wrong.

Even though the "R1" is incorrect, this paper showed that Reggie, Matthew, and Calie had divided the raisins correctly.

Sharing Raisens in the big box
We had 81 raisens.
We divided them by 20's and R1.

20   20   20

each person got 27

Matthew profited from working with this team. He stuck to the task until it was completed, and he got a view of division as something more than facts to carry around in his head.

A Class Discussion

In a class discussion, Lynne focused on two questions: "How did your group work together?" and "What were your results?" She had groups discuss both of these questions and also share the different ways they represented their work.

She then asked, "How did the number of raisins in the big box compare with the number of raisins in the small box?"

"There were more, lots more," Demetrius said.

"Like about two times," Keith added.

"I think there were more than two times more," Irene said.

"What are the sizes of the boxes?" Lynne asked.

"I tried matching them, but it was hard to tell," Truc said.

"Let's see what the net weights are for both," Lynne said. "That gives me a clue." She wrote on the board:

$$\text{Small box} - \tfrac{1}{2} \text{ ounce}$$
$$\text{Big box} - 1\tfrac{1}{2} \text{ ounces}$$

"There's one more in the big box," Courtney said.

"One more what?" Lynne probed. Courtney shrugged.

Aaron raised his hand. "The big box should have three times as much," he said. "It's $1\tfrac{1}{2}$ ounces, and that's $\tfrac{1}{2}$ ounce three times."

"I don't get it," Ashley said.

"Maybe that's right," Truc said. He had one of each box. "It's more than two, but the shape's not right." He was trying to compare the boxes.

"Let me see," Ethan said. Truc gave the boxes to him.

"Hmmm," he said. "This is tricky."

"From your papers, it seems that there were about 80 to 90 raisins in the big box," Lynne said.

"We had 97," Carey said.

"How many were in the small boxes?" Lynne asked. The children looked at the class chart.

"They went from 31 to 44," Gabrielle read.

Irene said, "That's two times with the littler number—no, more. Oooh, that's hard."

"It's three times," Aaron insisted.

This kind of proportional reasoning was out of the grasp of most of the children. And measurement, never being exact, didn't help. Lynne ended the discussion, but some of the children continued to talk among themselves about the numbers.

MENU ACTIVITY

Overview

Candy Box Family Guides

Working individually or in pairs, students create Candy Box Family Guides to help families decide what size boxes of candy to buy so they can share the candy equally among family members. Creating guides gives students experience thinking about how multiples of numbers relate to division. This activity was originally created as an extension of the *Candy Box Research* menu activity from the *Math By All Means: Multiplication, Grade 3* unit. (See the Bibliography, page 211.) In that activity, children connected multiplication to geometry by exploring how to pack 1-inch square tiles ("candies") one layer deep into rectangular arrays. However, children who have not worked on the multiplication activity can still benefit from this activity by focusing on the numbers of candies rather than on the rectangular arrays.

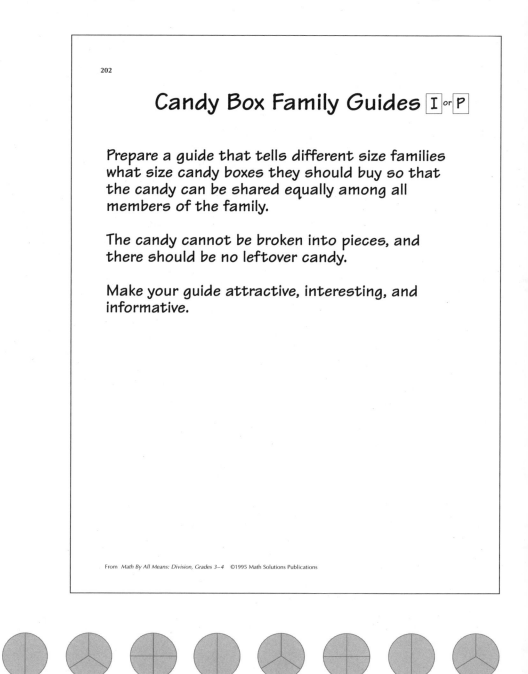

202

Candy Box Family Guides I or P

Prepare a guide that tells different size families what size candy boxes they should buy so that the candy can be shared equally among all members of the family.

The candy cannot be broken into pieces, and there should be no leftover candy.

Make your guide attractive, interesting, and informative.

From *Math By All Means: Division, Grades 3–4* ©1995 Math Solutions Publications

Before the lesson

Gather these materials:
■ One sheet of chart paper, entitled "Family Sizes in Our Class"
■ Blackline master of menu activity, page 202

Getting started

■ Post the chart entitled "Family Sizes in Our Class" and write the numbers 1 to 10 vertically. (You may have to number further if children have larger families.)

```
┌──────────────────────────────────────┐
│        Family Sizes in Our Class      │
│    1                                   │
│    2                                   │
│    3                                   │
│    4                                   │
│    5                                   │
│    6                                   │
│    7                                   │
│    8                                   │
│    9                                   │
│    10                                  │
│                                        │
│                                        │
└──────────────────────────────────────┘
```

■ Have each student write a tally mark on the chart to indicate the size of his or her family. Define the size of a family as the number of people who live in a student's house.

■ Present the following problem: People generally like to buy candy that they can share equally among everyone at their house. For example, if someone buys a box of six candies for a family with five people, there will be one extra candy, and this can cause a squabble.

■ Tell the children that they are to work individually or in pairs and write a guide for families who want to buy candy that they can share equally among all family members. The guide should provide the choice for each size family in the class.

■ Encourage children to make their guides attractive and informative. If children are familiar with the *Candy Box Research* activity from *Math By All Means: Multiplication, Grade 3*, they might choose to cut out rectangular boxes and paste them into their guides.

■ In a later class discussion, have students report the different numbers of candy possible for each size family and write the numbers on the board. Tell the children that these numbers are "multiples" of the family size and are "divisible" by the number in the family. Rewrite the numbers in ascending order (for example: *Divisible by 4: 4, 8, 12, 16, 20, 24, 28, 32*) and have children add numbers to continue the list.

FROM THE CLASSROOM

Lynne introduced *Candy Box Family Guides* by reminding students of their earlier experience with investigating candy boxes in the *Math By All Means: Multiplication, Grade 3* unit. They had arranged 1-inch tiles ("candies") into rectangular arrays for quantities of candies from 1 to 36.

"When people buy candies," Lynne said, "they have to decide how many to get. One way for them to decide is to choose a number of candies that they can share equally among all the members of their family."

Lynne then gave the children several problems to think about. First, she said, "What if there were five people in a family, and someone bought a box with 10 candies in it. Could they share them equally?"

"Yes," chorused the children.

"They'd each get two," Courtney added.

"What if the person bought a box with 12 candies?" Lynne then asked.

"It wouldn't work," Matthew said.

"There would be two extras," Irene said.

"The parents could have them," Truc added.

"But kids like candy better," Keith offered.

"There might be three kids," Aaron said. "Then there would be trouble."

"So it would be better if people bought the right number of candies so that everyone could have some," Lynne said. "How many candies could that be for a family of five? Talk with your neighbor about this and see what numbers would work."

After a minute, Lynne asked the children what they thought.

"We thought 5 or 10," Vivian reported for her and Justine.

"I think 15 works, too," Tano added.

"All the 5s would work," Aaron said, "like 5, 10, 15, 20, 25, like that."

"So there are many recommendations you could make for a family of five," Lynne said. "In this activity, you are to create a guide for families and give them several choices to help them decide which sizes of boxes would be good ones, so everyone could have the same number of candies. But first, we have to find out what sizes of families to consider."

Lynne posted the chart she had prepared entitled "Family Sizes in Our Class." She wrote the numbers from 1 to 10. "If we each put a tally mark on the chart next to the number that tells how many people are in our family, we'll have an idea about what to include in our guides. To figure out the size of your family, count all the people who live in your house. In my house, I live with my husband, so I'll put a tally mark next to the 2." Lynne did this to show the children how to record. Then she asked each child to come up and add a tally mark.

The chart revealed that the family size in their classroom ranged from one to eight. (Grandpa, the senior citizen volunteer who worked in the class once a week, lived alone.)

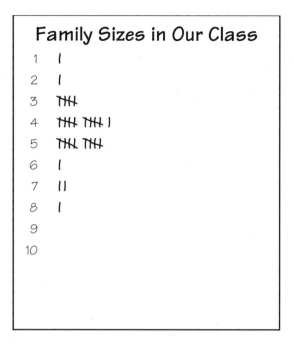

"So your guide has to give information about which sizes of boxes would work for each size family from one to eight people," Lynne said. "There may be families with more people, but we'll use the sample of our class for our guides."

Lynne then gave them some procedural information. "You may work alone or with a partner," she said. Lynne had constructed a booklet as a model for the children.

"Use the front page for a cover. Leave the other side of the cover blank and then use one page for each size family from one to eight. On the extra page at the end, you can solve an extra problem if you like by seeing if you can find one box that would work for families with two, three, four, five, and six people." Lynne referred to the written menu directions (see page 202) that she had enlarged and posted.

Observing the Children

As children worked on their guides, it became apparent that the initial focus of these TV-generation children was on the selling points of the manufacturer rather than on the needs of the family. The children spent a lot of time making fancy cover designs with slogans to entice; Samantha's and Brittany's were typical. (Their work appears on the next page.)

Aaron and Truc offered free boxes of candy in a best-for-less campaign. They wrote: *Buy 100 and get two for free.*

Gabrielle and Veronica made a multicolored cover decorated with hearts and moons and stars proclaiming: *Grand Opening: A Candy Store for All the People.* They continued the hearts-and-stars theme inside. For each size family, they offered the choice of small, medium, and large selections.

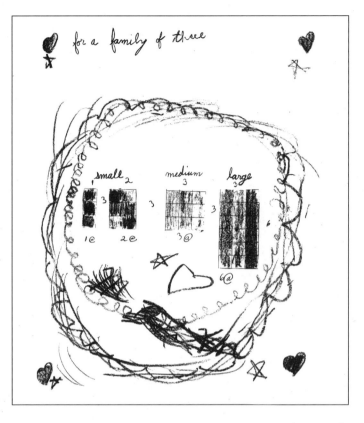

(above) Samantha used bold marker lines to display her advertisement.

(above right) Gabrielle and Veronica offered four choices for a family of three.

(right) Brittany's cover was a colorful enticement to customers.

Although Lynne had not planned that the *Candy Box Family Guides* would take such a commercial tone, she didn't try to stop the sales pitches. The children were reveling in imitating TV ads and in so doing were linking a division experience with their own worlds. Lynne knew that the final product was not the real test of learning. As always, she pushed for mathematics understanding during the process.

Several children's guides offered options. Justine and Ashley suggested different purposes for different sizes: *If your on a diet, use our 2 × 3 box. Having a party? use our 3 × 6 box.* They also offered five suggestions for a family of two.

Justine and Ashley had five suggestions for a family of two.

Other children enjoyed linking the numbers to social reality. Calie and Courtney designed six possible candy boxes for a family of one, including a 1-by-1 "low fat" box for Grandpa. For families of two, Calie and Courtney offered four possible boxes, including: *Going on a diet? Try our 1 × 2. Also nice for afternoon snacks.* Their guide said that the 3-by-2 box was *nice for desserts.*

Truc and Aaron, concerned with marketing ploys as they worked on their guide, offered free 4-by-7 boxes to families of four.

As she looked at their work, Lynne asked, "Who else could get this 4-by-7 box without argument? Could a family of two?"

Truc carefully counted squares on graph paper and said, "Yes, 14 pieces each."

"Could a family of three share it?"

"No." Aaron figured the answer in his head, while Truc counted squares. "There would be a remainder."

"Six people?" asked Lynne.

Truc replied, "Well, 6 plus 6 equals 12, and 6 more equals 18, plus 6 more is 24, plus 6 equals 30." He shook his head. "No, a family of six can't use it."

"So, which size families couldn't share a 4-by-7 box?" asked Lynne.

Truc and Aaron pondered this and then replied, "Families of three, five, six, and eight couldn't get it."

Truc and Aaron included a free offer for "candy lovers."

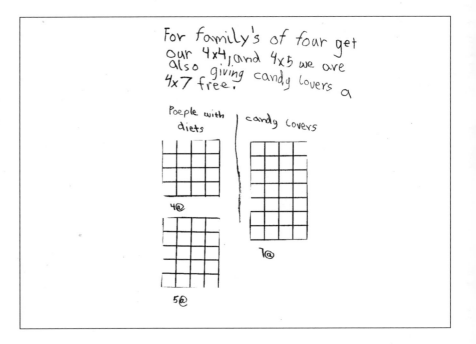

Garrett and Reggie worked well together until the end of the period, when Reggie wanted to put all their work in the "Copy" pocket of his folder. He pointed out that Lynne would photocopy it so they each would have a copy. Garrett knew how the system worked, but he wanted something in his folder at the end of the period.

"You take some; I'll take some. We'll both ask Mrs. Zolli for copies," he insisted. Reggie, who recognizes an immovable object when he sees it, agreed.

Jamie was one of seven children who solved the extra problem. Her last page read: *New! buy our new 60 piece candy box! It works for familys of 3, 4, 5, and 6!*

Jamie solved the extra problem of a candy box that worked for families of three, four, five, and six.

J. H. Candy CO

New! buy our new 60 piece candy box. It works for familys of 3, 4, 5, and 6!

Check it out! ↓

A Class Discussion

When Lynne called the class together for a discussion, she wasn't planning to have children share their guides. Rather, she wanted to focus on the mathematics and help the children connect their work to the ideas of multiples and divisibility.

However, Demetrius was eager to show the class what he had done, and Lynne allowed him to do so. Demetrius held up the guide's cover, on which he had proclaimed: *Delicious and expensive Quality candy. Buy 500 guides, 1 free trip to Bermuda Triangle swim there! No money back guarantee!* Then he wanted to read his price list to the class. He announced that he was selling 1-by-1 candy for $100 each. The class booed. Then Demetrius said that a 1-by-3 candy box sold for $200. Again, the children booed.

Calie asked, "Who would buy Demetrius's candy?"

Hugh announced, "I'll buy it!"

"Hugh is a millionaire," Reggie said.

Demetrius continued to read from his guide: *"You touch it, you buy it."* (Later, Lynne asked Demetrius to figure out the cost per piece in his $200 box. "That's your new job," she said. "Figure out how much each piece of your candy costs. The family needs to know.")

Lynne then asked the children to refer to their guides and report how many candies they recommended for a family of four. She gave them a moment to find the right page, and then called on children for their suggestions. "Don't tell your amount if someone else has already offered it," she told them. She wrote children's suggestions on the board as they offered them:

16, 20, 8, 4, 12, 28

"Help me write these numbers in order from smallest to largest," she said, after all children who wanted to had reported. She wrote the list again:

4, 8, 12, 16, 20, 28

"I think there's one number smaller than 28 that would work, but it's missing from the list," she said.

Aaron, Ethan, Matthew, and Irene raised their hands. Lynne called on Ethan. "It's 24," he said. Lynne added it, changing the 28 to 24, and then writing 28 again.

"Ooooh, we had that one," Justine said.

"What would be the next larger size box that would also work?" Lynne asked.

"You keep adding 4 more," Irene said, "so it would be . . . let's see . . . 31—no, 32."

"Then comes 36, and then 40," Truc added. Lynne added these to the list:

4, 8, 12, 16, 20, 24, 28, 32, 36, 40

"These numbers are all multiples of 4," she said, "that's why they work. We say that they are divisible by 4 because when you divide them by 4, there aren't any leftovers." Lynne wrote in front of the list:

Divisible by 4:

"Let's look at what's possible for families of five," she then said. "What's the smallest size box?"

"Five," several children answered in unison.

"And next?" Lynne asked, knowing that counting by 5s was easy for most of the children. She continued writing as children reported:

Divisible by 5: 5, 10, 15, 20, 25, 30, 35, 40, 45, 50

She did the same for 2s, knowing that this sequence was also easy for the children:

Divisible by 2: 2, 4, 6, 8, 10, 12, 14, 16, 18, 20

"They're all the even numbers!" Truc exclaimed, excited by his discovery.

Lynne continued for 3 and 6, and then ended the discussion.

ASSESSMENT Classroom Groups

FROM THE CLASSROOM

NOTE What to do with remainders depends on the situation. In this case, one way to deal with the remainder is to add the extra student to one of the groups, making a group of three.

This assessment gives children a real-world problem, one based on the kind of decisions that come up frequently in their own classroom.

Introduce the problem by asking the children to give reasons why you might want to put them in groups. After they have offered their ideas, introduce the problem. Ask, "If we put _____ students in our class into groups of 2, 3, 4, 5, 6, 7, 8, 9, and 10, how many groups would we have each time?"

Have the children determine the number of students in class. (Decide if you want the children to use the number in the class altogether or how many are present that day.) Then ask them how many groups there would be if they paired up into groups of two. Have several children explain their reasoning.

Tell the children they are to work individually to find answers and write about how they found them. Be sure they understand that they are to solve nine different problems and put the students into groups of 2, then 3, 4, 5, 6, 7, 8, 9, and 10.

As with most problems, children typically approach this problem in different ways. Some describe their solutions in writing; others prefer to draw diagrams. Some rely on addition; others use multiplication or subtraction. Some solve the problems by dividing the class into groups of 2, 3, 4, and so on; others divide the class into two groups, then three groups, four groups, and so on. The children's responses provide information for a rich classroom discussion.

"We've been putting a lot of things into equal groups these last few weeks—tiles, cookies, raisins," Lynne said to her students. "Sometimes teachers need to put children into groups. Can someone give a reason why I might want to put you into groups?"

"To work on problems together," volunteered Carey.

"Field trips," said Courtney.

Other children suggested, "To play a game." "To write stories."

"You get into groups for all sorts of reasons," agreed Lynne. "Sometimes I put you in large groups, sometimes small. Today we're going to work on a problem about groups. To do it, we need to know how many students are in our class today."

"Thirty," Reggie answered quickly.

"Two are absent," remembered Truc. "That makes 28."

"Yes," agreed Lynne. "And three are at speech, so how many are here right now?"

"Twenty-five," came a chorus of voices.

Lynne wrote *25* on the board. "If I took the 25 of you and put you into pairs, how many groups of 2 would we have?"

Truc volunteered, "I know! It's 12."

"Tell us how you figured out that answer."

"Well, 10 plus 10 equals 20. Five left over. Split them up, that makes two more groups and . . . ," he frowned and hesitated.

Irene offered, "It's 12, remainder 1."

"What will I do with the leftover student?" asked Lynne.

"One group gets three in it," said Irene.

NOTE When trying to connect mathematics with the real world, it's important not to ignore children's real-world concerns. It's a good idea to honor students' suggestions when they offer the same potential for children to think and reason mathematically.

NOTE Classroom procedures should not seem arbitrary to children. By respecting students enough to bring them in on the reasoning behind procedures, teachers have a better chance of gaining their full cooperation.

Reggie said, "I have another way!" He counted by 2s to 22, and Lynne listed the numbers on the board.

"Now what?" asked Lynne.

"Circle them," he directed.

After Lynne had done this, Reggie noticed, "I didn't go far enough. I left out 24." Lynne added 24. Reggie counted the numbers and said, "Twelve groups of 2 . . . with one remainder."

Lynne asked if anyone had a different way of thinking about the problem. No one did, so she introduced the assessment. "I'd like you to take a sheet of paper and show how we can put the 25 of you in these different groups." As she spoke, Lynne wrote on the board:

Classroom Groups
Mrs. Zolli wants to put her 25 students into groups of 2, 3, 4, 5, 6, 7, 8, 9, 10. How can she do this?

"Be sure to put your name and the date on your paper," she reminded, "along with this title and the problem."

Reggie worried, "What happens when the three people come back?" Since Lynne had modeled the problem with 25, she had planned to have the children continue with that number in their own problem solving. But she knew that Reggie's question was important. He was correct that the three students in the pullout program would return before the math period was over. Lynne felt that ignoring Reggie was like saying, "Never mind that you've just gone through the process of proving there are 28 children in our classroom today; let's just pretend it's 25 because that's the number I chose to work with." Lynne knew that the children would reveal their understanding and make interesting discoveries no matter which number they used, so she chose to honor Reggie's concern.

"You're right, Reggie," said Lynne. She erased the 25 and replaced it with a 28. To be sure all the students understood this change in the number, Lynne asked for a volunteer to explain how they were going to solve putting 28 students into groups of 2.

Courtney volunteered, "You take the 20 and break it into 10 and 10. Then take the 8 and break it into 4s. Add 10 + 4."

When Lynne asked the children to get to work, Gabrielle asked, "Can we work with partners?" Lynne usually allows children to work with partners, and she feels that when she insists they work alone, she should explain her reasons.

In this instance, Lynne shook her head "no," explaining that she would like the children to work alone. "Today I want each of you to have your own paper so I can see what you do to solve a problem," she said. "You can talk to people at your table, but I want you to do it your own way. This is important for me to see because you each have a special way to look at problems. I want to see Gabrielle's way, Aaron's way, Irene's way, Truc's way—and everybody else's way. I like the way you cooperate in groups, but sometimes it's important for me to see how each one of you thinks."

Ashley wrote the problem on her paper. Then she jumped up from her desk and told Lynne, "I need help." Asking for help immediately is Ashley's most frequently employed problem-solving strategy. Trying to reassure Ashley but refusing to shortcut her thinking, Lynne restated the problem.

"Oooh," smiled Ashley. "I get it."

Aaron told Lynne, "I'm going to kind of do it the way Truc did it."

"That's fine," confirmed Lynne. "If that way makes sense to you."

Reggie found this problem particularly engrossing right from the start. For each number, he listed multiples until he reached or passed 28, and then circled them. "I'm doing it like calculator patterns," he said, referring to a menu activity in the previous multiplication unit. His excitement grew as a chart emerged on his paper. "Wow!" he repeated over and over.

Reggie listed multiples to figure out how many groups there would be.

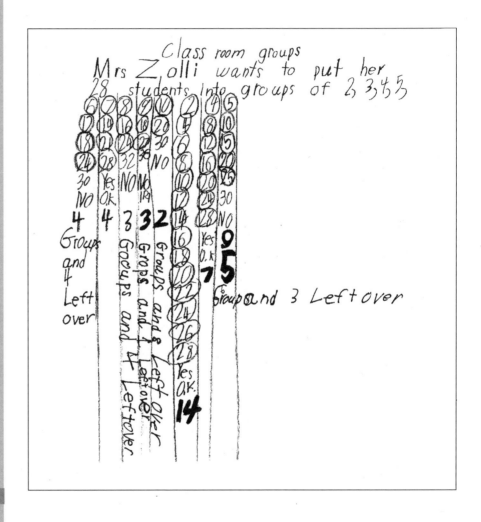

NOTE There are two different ways of thinking about a division problem. For example, 28 ÷ 2 can be interpreted as putting 28 into two groups, or as putting 28 into groups of 2. The answer in both situations is 14, but they have different interpretations: 2 groups with 14 children in each or 14 groups with 2 children in each. Considered abstractly, both have the same numerical answer, but the meaning of the numerical answer is different when explained in terms of each context.

Two minutes into the assignment, Calie rushed up to Lynne. "I know how you can split it one way," she said. "See, there are 28 kids, and that's 14 plus 14." She was very pleased. Lynne wasn't sure if Calie was thinking about students in groups of 2, or about putting them into two groups. She didn't respond, however, but waited to see how Calie would approach the other problems.

When she was finished, Calie's paper revealed that her strategy for each problem was to draw 28 circles, and then circle groups of 2, 3, 4, etc., to put the students into groups. Calie was able to use the symbolism of division correctly, but she miscounted once, and didn't have time to finish.

Calie's strategy was to draw 28 circles and group them.

After dividing 28 by 2 numerically, Gabrielle solved the rest of the problems by arranging circles into groups of 3, 4, 5, and so on.

Gabrielle also drew circles, but she organized them into groups of 2, 3, 4, etc. Lynne made a note to discuss the different interpretations later with the class.

Ethan is admired by his classmates for his complex, detailed, and humorous narratives. Because this was a real-world problem using groupings for his own class, Ethan gave each remainder an explanation, ranging from *send the remaining students home* to *let the student help the teacher* to *throw him out the window and let him play*. Ethan's detailed paper contrasted with the sparcity of his work at the beginning of this unit and probably reflected the seriousness with which he reacted to Lynne's recent private conversation with him about assuming responsibility for completing his work.

Ethan had a variety of suggestions for what to do with extra students.

Classroom Groups

Mrs. Zolli wants to put her 28 students into groups of 2, 3, 4, 5, 6, 7, 8, 9, 10. can she do this ???
28÷2=14, 28÷3=9 R1 I would send the remaining students home. 29÷4=7 28÷5=5 R3 I would let the remaining children wait. 28÷6=3 R1 I would let the student help the teacher. 28÷7=3 R1 I would throw him out the window and let him play. 28÷8 Each group would get 7 students. 28÷9=3 R1 I would let him do something different.

Ethan's "throw him out the window" idea quickly spread around the room and was repeated on other papers. Aaron used the idea throughout his paper. However, he changed the total number of students each time to reflect how many were left after some were out the window. By the time Aaron got to the last problem of making groups of 10, he had only 9 students left. He wrote: *Get a kid to enroll and ÷ 10 by 10.*

Aaron changed 28 to numbers that would result in no remainders.

Mrs Zolli wants to put her student into groups of 2, 3, 4, 5, 6, 7, 8, 9, 10 How can she do this ???

2
20
10 10
4   4
14 14

3
Throw 1 out the window and ÷ 27 by 3. 3, 6, 9, 12, 15, 18, 21, 24, 27. ÷ 3

5
Throw two kids out the windo and ÷ 25 by 5. 5, 10, 15, 20, 25 ÷
Throw 1 kid out the window and ÷ 24 by

27 Kids Throw 3 kids out the window and ÷ 24 by 4. 4, 8, 12, 16, 20, 24.

6, 12, 18, 24, ÷

Throw 3 kids and ÷ 21 by 7. 7, 14, 21.

Throw 5 more kids out the window and ÷ 16 by 8. 8, 16.

Throw 7 kids out the window and ÷ 9 by 9. 9.

Get a kid to enroll and ÷ 10 by 10. 10.

Kent used the same 28 faces to figure out the answer to each problem, but he made two division errors.

Kent drew 28 faces and used them over and over again to make groups to figure out the answers. He recorded his answers using standard symbolism, but in two instances he wrote incorrect answers: *28 ÷ 3 = 27 R1* and *28 ÷ 5 = 25 R1*. In each example, the incorrect answer had some mathematical connection to the problem; it was the multiple of the divisor that came just before 28.

Truc's solutions show his understanding of the relationship between multiplication and division.

Truc used what he knew about multiplication to solve the problems, noting that 9 × 3 and 3 × 9 are *just switcharouds and they are the same. One means 9 groups of 3 and 3 groups of 9.* When asked, "Are they really the same?" Truc replied, "One has more different groups but it's the same number total."

A Class Discussion

Lynne called the children to the floor at the front of the room and said, "I'm going to show you some things, and I'd like to see if you can explain what I'm doing. Actually, what I'm putting on the board is what you did yesterday."

Lynne drew 28 circles on the board, then turned to the class and asked, "What have I done so far?"

"Made heads," answered the class.

"How many?"

"Twenty-eight."

Lynne circled the 28 heads in groups of 3s.

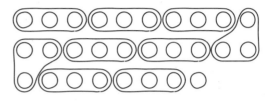

"I drew this the way it appeared on one of your papers," Lynne said. "Who can explain what this girl did?"

"She circled every three," volunteered Keith.

"What's the mathematical sentence?"

"I think it's 28 divided by 3 equals 9 remainder 1," he said. Lynne wrote:

$$28 \div 3 = 9\,R1$$

"How did she figure the number of groups of three?" asked Lynne.

"She counted circles. Nine circles," said Courtney.

"I'd like to give credit to Calie for the thinking in this problem," smiled Lynne. "Now I'm going to draw a different way of thinking about the same thing."

1	2	3
○ ○	○ ○	○ ○
○ ○	○ ○	○ ○
○ ○	○ ○	○ ○
○ ○	○ ○	○ ○
○	○	○

"Who can explain this thinking?" she asked.

Truc explained, "It's three groups of nine. But that's only 27."

"What about the mathematical sentence?" prompted Lynne. Truc repeated what Keith had offered for Calie's solution.

"I'd like to give credit to Gabrielle for this thinking," Lynne said, and turned to write on the board again.

"This next one is interesting, and I don't want the person who did it to give the method away," she cautioned. She drew a sample from Reggie's solution. (See page 127.) In his paper, Reggie had inadvertently skipped solving the problem of putting students into groups of three. Lynne, therefore, chose to record the way he solved the problem of putting students into groups of four. She listed the multiples of 4, stopping at 28.

"Oooh!" children gasped in awe, amazement, and growing understanding.
"What are you thinking?" asked Lynne.
"That's times and division," said Irene.
Lynne continued writing other lists of multiples as Reggie had done, adding "YES" or "NO" at the end of each column.

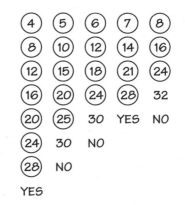

There were more "ooohs," as children saw more patterns. They waved their hands excitedly, wanting to talk about their revelations. "I know what he did!" "So do I!"
Lynne continued to wait before calling on anyone. Excitement grew, as more children gained understanding. Lynne gave time for the children to recognize the pattern, time for all children to think. The entire class was intent on studying the board.
Finally, Lynne asked, "What do you notice?"
"The pattern gets shorter and shorter," Brittany said.
Lynne pointed to the list of multiples of 5 and asked, "What does he mean by 'NO'?"
Irene said, "There's extras, leftovers."
Ashley asked, "Why did he say yes on 4?"
"It came out perfectly, no leftovers," Irene explained.

Demetrius's paper showed how he connects addition and division.

"I'd like to thank Reggie for this thinking," said Lynne. "Did you want to explain some more to us, Reggie?"

Reggie grinned, "I did it like calculator patterns. I used my mind like a calculator." Reggie uses this metaphor often. He says that imagining his mind as a calculator helps him solve "hard math."

Lynne added, "Reggie thought of solving the problem of dividing the class into equal groups by using what he knows about multiplication." She reviewed the patterns in Reggie's scheme and invited the class to add the others she had not written. Then Lynne asked the question that she asks more than any other. "Did anyone think about this problem in a different way?"

Aaron said, "I did it like Reggie, but in words. When I did groups of five, I started out by throwing three kids out the window, so then I could count by 5s to 25."

Courtney commented, "Wouldn't that be murder?"

"It wasn't a high window," answered Aaron.

Lynne said, "I always like to prove something before I believe it. We found out that 28 divided by 5 equals 5, remainder 3. Arrange yourselves into groups of five and sit down together. Then we'll check."

"But we're all here today," Kent said.

"Then two of you will be helpers to help me prove the answer," Lynne said, and picked Wesley and Justine.

After the intensity of "getting inside" one another's thinking, the physical activity of making these groups was a welcome relief. With a lot of laughter and friendly nudging, the students eventually grouped themselves and "proved" the equation: Three children stood as "remainders."

Classroom Groups

Mrs. Zolli wants to put her 28 students into groups of 2, 3, 4, 5, 6, 7, 8, 9, 10. How can she do this???

2. She can divide 28 students into 14 groups of 2. $14 \times 14 = 28$

3. She can divide 28 students into 9 groups of 3 and throw the leftover person out the window $3+3+3+3+3 = 3 \times 9 = 3 \times 3 = 27$ $27+1 = 28$

4. She can divide 28 students into 7 groups of 4. $4+4+4+4+4+4+4 = 28$

5. She can divide 28 students into 5 groups of 5 and throw 3 people out the window! $5+5+5+5+5 = 25$ $25+3 = 28$

6. She can divide 28 students into 4 groups of 6 and throw 4 people out the window. $6+6+6+6 = 24$ $24+4 = 28$

7. She can divide 28 students into 4 groups of 7 $7+7+7+7 = 28$

8. She can divide 28 students into 3 groups of 8 and throw 4 people out the window. $8+8+8 = 24$ $24+4 = 28$

9. She can divide 28 students into 3 groups of 9 and throw 1 person out the window $9+9+9 = 27$ $27+1 = 28$

10.

Lynne then challenged the students to rearrange themselves into groups of seven and report the result in conventional mathematical symbolism.

After this, Lynne had the students begin work on menu activities. Irene asked Lynne if she could redo her work on the grouping problem. "I could do it better," she said. She was particularly impressed by Gabrielle's and Reggie's solutions and felt inspired to create one of her own. When Lynne agreed that she could do it again, Irene announced, "And I'm going to work by myself." She moved her supplies to an isolated corner of the room and got started.

Wesley solved the problems in a unique way.

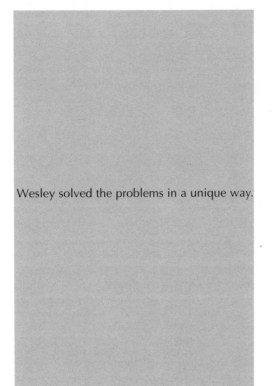

MENU ACTIVITY

Overview

17 Kings and 42 Elephants

Margaret Mahy's book *17 Kings and 42 Elephants* employs playful, rhythmic language in the context of a royal procession through an exotic jungle. In this menu activity, students enjoy the book for its vibrant batik illustrations and semantic delights. The story then becomes a springboard for a division problem with remainders, which the students solve individually or in pairs.

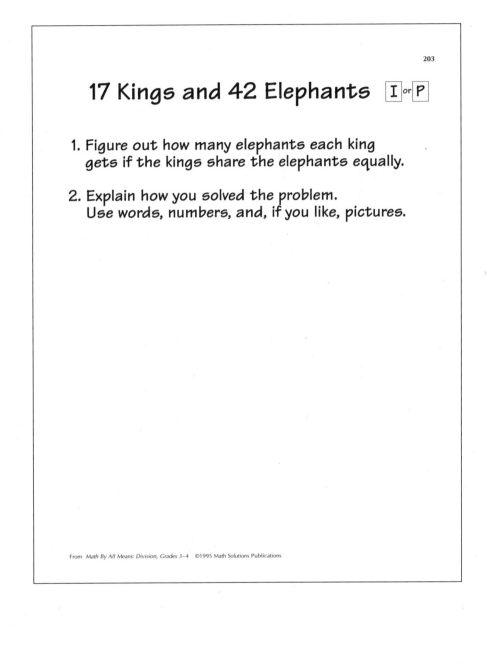

203

17 Kings and 42 Elephants $\boxed{\text{I}}$ or $\boxed{\text{P}}$

1. Figure out how many elephants each king gets if the kings share the elephants equally.

2. Explain how you solved the problem. Use words, numbers, and, if you like, pictures.

From *Math By All Means: Division, Grades 3–4* ©1995 Math Solutions Publications

Before the lesson

Gather these materials:
- ■ *17 Kings and 42 Elephants* by Margaret Mahy (See Children's Books section, page 187.)
- ■ Blackline master of menu activity, page 203

Getting started

■ Read the story aloud to the class. The book describes a royal procession of 17 kings and 42 elephants through an exotic jungle. The language is infectiously rhythmic and the illustrations are a visual delight.

■ Introduce the problem. Ask students to work individually or in pairs to determine how many elephants each king would get if the kings shared them equally. Tell students to write about how they solved the problem.

■ In a later class discussion, have students share their solutions with the class.

FROM THE CLASSROOM

Lynne introduced the activity by announcing to the class that she had a new book to share. She encouraged the children to savor the language and the art as she read aloud *17 Kings and 42 Elephants*. Courtney noted that "Baggy ears like big umbrellaphants" sounded like the words in "Eletelephony," a poem she had read. Lynne agreed that poets like to play with words and even invent them.

Truc asked Lynne to turn back to a double-page spread. This child, who is precise in his own work, wanted to make sure the artist had shown 17 kings on the two pages.

"Yes," he confirmed with a grin. "There are 17."

When she had finished reading the book, and the children had shared their reactions to the language and art, Lynne focused the class on the mathematical potential in the story. She asked, "How many kings were there?"

"Seventeen!" the children chorused.

"How many elephants?"

"Forty-two!"

"Subtraction!" exclaimed a half dozen children, confident they were anticipating Lynne's next question.

"We could do that," agreed Lynne. "We could ask: How many more elephants are there than kings?" She paused for a moment, as she noticed some children starting to solve that problem.

Several figured quickly that the answer was 25.

"There's another problem we might consider," Lynne commented, as she started writing on the board. "How many elephants did each king get?"

"Uh-oh." This classroom murmur was followed by individual speculations: "Seventeen plus seventeen." "Five each." "No, six."

Lynne asked, "Will each king get an elephant?"

"Yes, five," responded Ashley.

"No, seven each," Reggie quickly corrected her.

Lynne didn't comment about whether either student was right or wrong. She said what she says so often, "You'll need to decide and then show on paper how you figured it out. The problem is to figure out how many elephants each king would get if they shared them equally. Your solution should explain how you reasoned."

Lynne then gave directions about how the students might work. "If you think you want to discuss this with someone else, then you can work with a partner. Or you may work alone if you'd prefer."

Observing the Children

Aaron and Demetrius decided to work together. Aaron got a calculator and punched in 42 ÷ 17. When he saw 2.4705882 for an answer, this boy, who had correctly interpreted the decimal answer .25 in the *Explorations with Raisins* whole class lesson, was startled.

"What does it mean?" he asked Demetrius, who, along with Aaron, is recognized by his classmates as one of the best math students in the class. Demetrius shrugged his shoulders.

Aaron and Demetrius then went to Lynne. "We have no idea what the answer means," Aaron said, showing her the calculator.

"If your answer doesn't make sense," she suggested, "then try doing it another way."

Aaron sighed. Lynne decided to talk with them about the frustrations sometimes provided by calculator answers.

"Show me what you did," she said. Demetrius punched in 42 ÷ 17 and again got 2.4705882. Both boys groaned.

"Does any part of this number make sense?" prodded Lynne.

"Nooo," chorused the boys.

"Hey wait, the 2 makes sense!" exclaimed Demetrius.

"What do you think the 2 tells you about the problem?" Lynne asked.

"I know," Aaron said. "It means that 42 divided by 17 is 2."

"But that's not right," Demetrius said, "or else it would just say 2."

Lynne explained about decimals, that they gave a way to represent a number that was bigger than 2 but less than 3, and that students must learn how to interpret these numbers in order to use them. "In the meantime," she said, "you'll need to think about another way to solve the problem." Aaron looked glum.

"I know!" Demetrius said. "Let's get tiles." The boys returned to their seats.

Justine and Calie, frustrated by what to do with the calculator, asked for help. Lynne offered no immediate answer but posed a question to help them focus on the problem. "Are there too many kings or too many elephants?" She left the girls to ponder this question.

Later, when Lynne returned, Justine told her, "We think each king gets three elephants."

"Okay, check it out. Write down a 3. That 3 means three elephants for one king. Now write down another 3. That takes care of elephants for how many kings?"

"Two," said Justine.

"How many 3s do you need to write down to check your answer?" Lynne asked.

"Seventeen," Calie answered.

"And what do 17 groups of 3s equal?" Lynn asked.

Justine grabbed a calculator and punched in 17 × 3. "Fifty-one," she reported. "Too much."

Calie suggested, "How about 2?" She wrote the numeral 2 on her paper 17 times.

"There's another way," insisted Justine. She punched 2 × 17 into the calculator. When 34 appeared, Calie moaned, "Oh, that's not right either." Calie, for whom numbers are only right or wrong, has no notion of how to look at a remainder. But she is conscientious and willing to keep working. Her method is to keep trying numbers until she gets the one that she is looking for. If one number doesn't work, then she'll try another—without taking any time to think about why a number is incorrect. In this case, she did not look at whether 34 was too large or too small; all she noticed was that it wasn't 42.

Calie suggested, in more of a question than a hypothesis, "Maybe it's 1?" She quickly started writing down a row of 1s.

But Justine stopped her. "No, 34 is okay. That leaves 8 elephants left over." She grinned. "We can have the kings cut up the remainder." Justine was clearly the strength in this partnership. Nonetheless, she did not feel put upon or dragged down by Calie's lack of number sense. In explaining her own thinking to Calie, Justine clarified what she herself knew.

Stopping to talk with Cynthia, Lynne asked, "What are you going to do with the leftover elephants?"

Kent overheard from a nearby table. "Make elephant stew," he quipped.

"Feed them to the tigers," said Ethan, sitting next to Kent.

Lynne commented, "If you're going to use a mean solution, you need a nice one, too. Animal rights people will be upset if you are unkind to elephants."

Ethan obliged and included two possible scenarios. He wrote:

$$17 \div 42 = 2\ R8 \qquad 17\overline{)42}^{\,2\,R8}$$

I would say that each king should get two elephant and let the rest eight elephants free.

Mean Sulution: We will feed the eight remaining elephants to tigers and crocodiles. (Although part of his symbolism was reversed, his answer was right.)

Ethan provided two scenarios for what he might do with the extra elephants.

But Keith liked the tiger solution. He wrote: *Give the elephants to the tigers.* He decided there were five tigers and used his calculator to divide the eight remaining elephants among the five tigers. He wrote: *There were 5 tigers so each tiger gets 1.6 elephants.*

"How are you going to decide how much '.6 elephant' is?" challenged Ethan from a nearby table.

Keith answered, "Get a ruler." They both laughed, recognizing and appreciating the joke of misapplied mathematical tools.

Courtney had a more humane touch in her solution. She wrote: *Each king would get two elephants. The eight elephants that are left* [go] *to the tigers as slaves and tell the tigers not to eat them.*

Lynne commented to her, "You need to show how you figured that out." Courtney added: *I got this answer by adding 17 + 17, and 8 were left over.*

Gabrielle explained the problem of the leftover elephants: *We can not cut out the elephants. So I will gave the left over elephants to the zoo.* Her picture showed the 17 kings walking away from the zoo, where they had left eight (sad) elephants. "They don't like being left behind," Gabrielle explained.

Tano wrote, *If there* [are] *8 Elephants I will get 8* [new] *kings. then it is fair.*

Kent corrected him, "If there were 8 elephants I would get 4 more kings. Then it would be fair."

When Lynne checked on Reggie and Garrett, Reggie insisted, "Each king gets 7 elephants."

"Let's see," said Lynne. "Show me your thinking." Since Lynne says this all the time, it is not one of those red flag phrases that warns students they have made a mistake. She helped Reggie and Garrett construct the following chart:

7 elephants = 1 king
14 elephants = 2 kings
21 elephants = 3 kings
28 elephants = 4 kings
35 elephants = 5 kings
42 elephants = 6 kings

"Wow!" exclaimed Reggie, admiring the chart. But his admiration was short-lived. "Uh-oh, I'm in trouble. I didn't use up enough kings."

"If there were six kings, that would work," said Lynne, emphasizing the six.

"The solution is the others didn't want to be kings," suggested Reggie.

Garrett liked this solution. "They were probably scared of elephants," he added.

"Okay, write it up," agreed Lynne.

Later Lynne acknowledged, "In the days of workbook or textbook problems, that would have been a wrong answer. But I'm not looking for mass-produced questions or answers. I'm trying to recognize and nurture children's thinking. Here are two boys who have difficulty in school. They are struggling to make sense of a difficult concept. Reggie recognizes his answer isn't right, which is a profound recognition for him. So when he comes up with this clever solution for getting himself out of a numerical jam, I want to celebrate his humor, not stamp it 'wrong answer.'"

Lynne paused. "And, for a bonus, Reggie kept Garrett right along with him. Every day I am frustrated that I can give so little help to Garrett, who needs so much help." An active participant in class discussions, Garrett has profound difficulties in reading, writing, and mathematics. On a typical school day his written work ranges from nothing to very little. So when he handed in a solution to the elephant problem, one that he had helped find, Lynne felt Garrett enjoyed some success.

What's important to Lynne is that she listen to the children's thinking and help them verbalize their reasoning. The point is not merely getting answers but how children arrive at those answers and communicate what they know to others.

At another table, Lynne asked Hugh to explain his thinking. Hugh said, "Each king would get two elephants."

"Any leftovers?" asked Lynne.

"No."

"How many elephants do you have?"

"I've got 42."

"But you only used 34."

Hugh counted on his fingers. "Eight elephants left over."

"That's good that you did it all in your head," Lynne said. "Now you need to write it down, so I can see your thinking."

A Class Discussion

After all of the students had found solutions to the problem, Lynne gathered them at the front of the room to share their thinking. She began by repeating something she says often when initiating a discussion: "Even though there is only one answer, there are many ways to get it. I'm interested in having you hear all the different ways you used."

Irene went first. She had drawn 15 elephant heads and then started using numbers to represent elephants up to 42. She drew slashes in one direction for 17 of the elephants and another direction for another 17. (Her work appears on the facing page.)

Irene was pleased that the teacher and other students were startled by her solution of feeding the leftover elephants to the lions. This is a child who explains that her mother gave her a name meaning peace "because she was born and grew up in Vietnam, which was a war place. My dad lived there too. My mom hoped that the whole world would like my peaceful name." She is also an independent child who doesn't want to be predictable. She prefers to work alone because, in her words, "Then there's no argument."

The children had different ways of arriving at the answer. Jamie showed her system of using tally marks and circles. (Her work appears on the facing page.)

Brittany demonstrated how she subtracted 17 twice to get the answer. (See page 142.)

Truc commented to Brittany, "Ours are sort of the same—but backwards," he said. He explained how he added 2 17 times. (Truc's work appears below Brittany's on page 142.)

To solve the problem, Irene used numbers and slashes.

17 Kings
42 Elephants

How could the kings share the elephant between them fairly?

@ king got 2 elephants @ and there would be 8 leftover and they gave the leftover elephants to the lions.

Jamie explained her system of circling tally marks.

17 Kings & 42 Elephants

How could the kings share the elephants between them fairly?

@ Each king would get two elephants @ and there would be eight leftover.

What the kings did with the leftover elephants was put them in the zoo.

We gave each king two elephants by drawing tally marks.
Kings | | | | | | | | | | | | | | | | |

Elephants

Brittany subtracted to figure out
the answer.

17 Kings and 42 Elephants

How could the
kings share the elepha-
nts between then
fairly?

$$4\overset{e}{2} - 1\overset{k}{7} = 2\overset{e}{5}$$
$$2\overset{e}{5} - 1\overset{k}{7} = \overset{e}{8}$$

Truc used addition to solve the problem.

17 King 42 elephants
How could king share the elephants
between them farly?

42 elephants

17 king

@ king gets two elephants @ because the other paper
proves it because that makes 34 and 8 leftovers.
Put them it the castle.

$$
\begin{array}{r}
2 \\
2 \\
2 \\
2 \\
2 \\
2 \\
2 \\
2 \\
2 \\
2 \\
2 \\
2 \\
2 \\
2 \\
2 \\
2 \\
+ 2 \\
\hline
34 \text{ and } 8 \text{ Leftover} = 42
\end{array}
$$

Brenna offered an unusual solution for the leftover elephants. "I added 17 plus 17 and got 34," she explained. "That means there are 8 leftovers. I think it would be fair to rotate the leftover elephants." She had written: *The kings can share 8 elephants. Eight kings can each have one elephant from the leftovers. The next day another 8 kings can get one leftover then another.*

Aaron, who had followed Brenna's argument carefully, objected, "Then one king would get one elephant by himself. That's not fair sharing."

Brenna was frustrated, unsure of how to answer Aaron. Lynne volunteered, "You're right, Aaron. On the first day, eight kings each get an extra elephant; then on the second, eight different kings get the extras; but on the third day there is only one king left who hasn't had an extra elephant. But he can get his turn along with seven kings who already had an extra elephant on the first day and can have extras again." Lynne illustrated this explanation with a diagram.

"I get it," smiled Aaron. "That's neat." Brenna grinned.

Brenna decided that the extra elephants should rotate among the kings.

> 17 King and 42 elephants
>
> How could the kings share the elephants between them fairly.
>
> There were 42 elephants & 17 kings.
>
> $$\begin{array}{r} 17 \\ + 17 \\ \hline 34 \text{ elephants} \end{array}$$
>
> Each king would get 2 elephants and there are 8 elephants leftover. The kings can share 8 elephants. Eight kings can have one elephant from the leftovers. The next day another 8 kings can get one leftover, then another.

"Reggie and Garrett have a different solution," said Lynne, wanting to give status to the two boys for the thinking they did. Reggie grinned as he announced, "Six kings got seven elephants each." He paused, "That's 42 elephants because 6 times 7 equals 42. We used a calculator."

"But that's only 6 kings!" protested several children.

"Because 11 kings were scared and didn't want any elephants," announced Garrett, offering their punchline. He and Reggie laughed, enjoying having surprised their classmates. Other children joined in the

laughter, also enjoying this method of turning a mathematics problem into a shaggy dog story.

The children were engrossed in this problem. They were intent on examining the thinking and problem-solving processes of their peers. They were anxious both to communicate what they knew and to learn from what their classmates knew.

It was nearly time to end math class and Lynne asked, "Are there any more solutions?" Kent volunteered.

"I had eight leftover elephants," he said, "and so I got four more kings. That means I have a new story. It's called '21 Kings and 42 Elephants.'"

Lynne smiled. "That's great! Two new stories: Kent's is '21 Kings and 42 Elephants.' Reggie and Garrett's is '6 Kings and 42 Elephants.'"

After they abandoned the calculator, Aaron and Demetrius used tiles to solve the problem.

MENU ACTIVITY

Overview

Sharing Candy Bars

In *Sharing Candy Bars,* children work in pairs to figure out how to share five rectangular "candy bars" equally among four people. Each candy bar is scored into six pieces. The problem presents an opportunity for children to think about fractions as they solve a division problem.

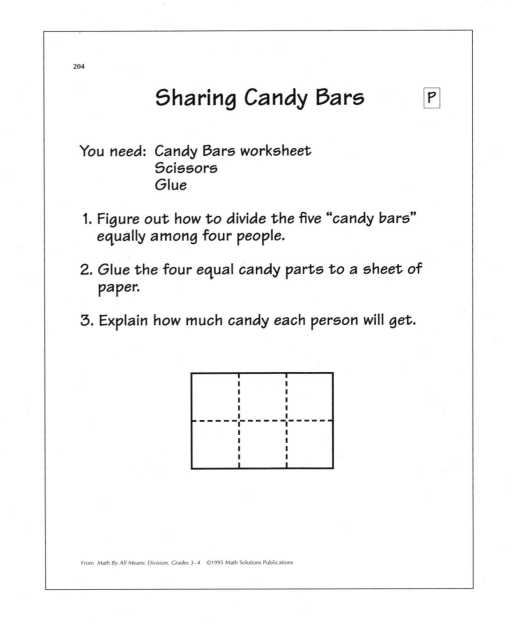

204

Sharing Candy Bars   P

You need: Candy Bars worksheet
Scissors
Glue

1. Figure out how to divide the five "candy bars" equally among four people.

2. Glue the four equal candy parts to a sheet of paper.

3. Explain how much candy each person will get.

From *Math By All Means: Division, Grades 3–4*   ©1995 Math Solutions Publications

Before the lesson

Gather these materials:
■ Blackline master of menu activity, page 204
■ Candy Bars worksheet, one per pair of students (See Blackline Masters section, page 205.)
■ Scissors
■ Glue

Getting started

■ Tell the children they are going to work in pairs to figure out how to share five "candy bars" equally among four people.

■ Hold up the Candy Bar worksheet and explain that each complete rectangle represents a candy bar. Tell the children that they should cut the "candy bars" as needed, decide how to divide them equally among four people, glue the portions to a sheet of paper, and finally write down how much each person's share is.

■ In a later class discussion, students share their solutions, their methods for finding them, and the ways they represented each person's share.

FROM THE CLASSROOM

To introduce the activity, Lynne said to the class, "*Sharing Candy Bars* presents a problem that is like the *Dividing Cookies* activity we did a few weeks ago."

"I bet they're just pretend candy bars," Hugh said.

"Yes, they are," Lynne confirmed and showed the children the Candy Bars worksheet on which there were five rectangular "candy bars," each scored into six squares.

"Your task is to figure out how to divide the five 'candy bars' among four people so that each gets a fair share," she continued. Because the children had experience sharing "cookies," they needed no further explanation.

"Can we work together?" Brenna wanted to know.

Lynne showed them the directions for the menu task. "Oh, yeah," Brenna said, noticing the P in the corner.

Observing the Children

Wesley and Keith decided to work together. They immediately set themselves the task of cutting apart all the squares. It took a long time. Keith became tired of cutting, and while Wesley continued to cut, Keith started dealing out squares, "Two for you and two for me." When the boys remembered that they were supposed to share these among four people, Wesley began numbering the squares: 1 2 3 4, 1 2 3 4.

"The answer is $7\frac{1}{2}$," Wesley announced.

Keith asked, "Are you sure?"

Wesley nodded and so Keith wrote: *Each person gets $7\frac{1}{2}$.* They took their paper to Lynne.

Lynne queried, "$7\frac{1}{2}$ what?" In this case, a possibly correct number masked an incorrect answer.

"Candy bars," answered the boys.

Lynne did not say "right" or "wrong." Instead, she asked, "How many candy bars did you start with?"

"Five," answered Wesley. Both boys said, "Uh-oh." Wesley and Keith are able students; they expect answers to make sense and, given a slight nudge, they can recognize incongruity.

Wesley and Keith returned to their table. They used scissors to cut off the first answer and, after a bit of figuring, wrote: *Each person gets 1 bar and ⅙ and a half of a sixth.* They were pleased that they knew what one-sixth was and how to write it.

Keith described how he and Wesley solved the problem.

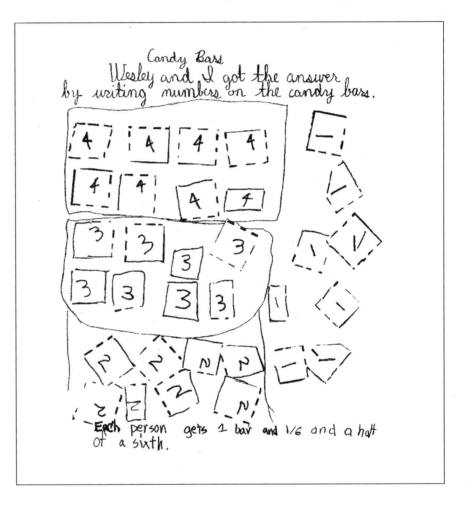

Samantha and Courtney also used a numbering system, but they did not use fractions to describe each person's share. They dealt out four of the candy bars whole, before they started cutting. Then they cut up the remaining bar, giving one square to each of four people. They cut the two remaining pieces in half and finally pasted all the pieces down.

The girls then began to write about their solution. Samantha and Courtney were convinced they had solved the problem "in our head." They were becoming familiar with fractions but were not yet naming parts. (Their work appears on the next page.)

Samantha and Courtney's solution was correct, but they did not use fractional symbols to describe each person's share.

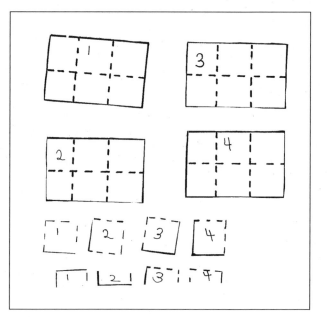

Candy Bars
Each person will get
1 whole candy bar, one
sqaure and a half of a
sqaure. We found this
out in our head.

Calie and Gabrielle started by cutting each candy bar in half. But they then got stuck, distracted by the lines on the candy bars. Lynne sat with them, helping them keep track of what a whole candy bar looked like. They glued their cut candy bars back together and decided that they needed four of them whole. Then they cut up the remaining candy bar—and discovered twelfths.

Calie and Gabrielle described twelfths.

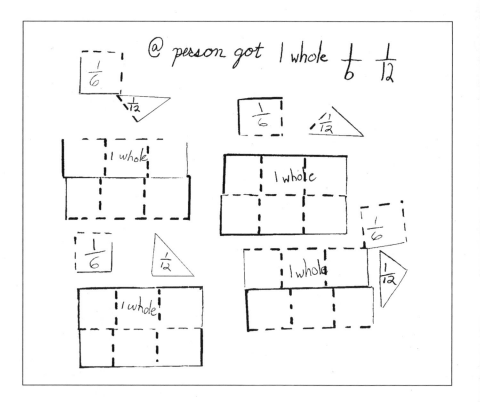

Before noticing that each person would get a whole candy bar, Patricia and Brittany cut four squares off each and pasted them down. Then they pasted an additional two squares for each person.

"That was dumb," Brittany said. "They each get one whole." As others had done, they then gave each person another square and a half of a square. Unlike Calie and Gabrielle, however, they did not use twelfths. They recorded each person's share as $1 + \frac{1}{6} + \frac{1}{2}$ of $\frac{1}{6}$.

Brittany recorded that she and Patricia gave each person $1 + \frac{1}{6} + \frac{1}{2}$ of $\frac{1}{6}$.

me and Patricia gave one Candy Bar one square and one half of a square that way they each have an equall amont of Candy. You can also do it like this $1+\frac{1}{6} + \frac{1}{2}$ of $\frac{1}{6}$

Matthew and Irene were working together. "Look," Irene said, "it's easy. They each get a whole bar, then a piece, and then half a piece."

Matthew agreed and began to record. "How about saying we did it in our heads?" he asked Irene.

Irene said, "Okay, I'll cut them up."

While Irene cut the pieces, Matthew wrote: *We just devided it in our head.* Then he drew four figures and pictured each with one candy bar, a piece, and half of a piece. Finally, Matthew wrote: *Each person gets 7¹/₂.* The two children took their solution to Lynne.

As she had done with Wesley and Keith, Lynne asked, "7¹/₂ what?"

"Little pieces," Irene said. "See?" She showed Lynne what she meant.

"You need to be more specific in your sentence," Lynne said. "Someone could think you meant 7¹/₂ candy bars."

They went back and added *pieces of candy* to their last sentence. Then they refined it further, ending up with: *Each person gets 7¹/₂ individual pieces of candy.*

Matthew and Irene reported how many small squares each person got.

> Sharing Candy Bars
>
> 1. We just devided it in our head
>
> 2.
>
> 3. Each person gets 7 ½ individual pieces of candy.

A Class Discussion

In a later class discussion, the students reported their solutions and how they had represented them. Lynne recorded on the board as they reported:

$7\frac{1}{2}$ individual pieces

$1 + \frac{1}{6} + \frac{1}{2}$ of $\frac{1}{6}$

1 and $\frac{1}{6}$ and a half of a sixth

$1\frac{1}{4}$

1 whole $\frac{1}{6}$ $\frac{1}{12}$

1 candy bar and $\frac{3}{12}$

"What do you think of all these different solutions?" Lynne asked.
"It's neat," Truc said. "There's lots of ways."
"Are they all right?" Vivian wanted to know.
"Do they make sense?" Lynne asked. She rarely says whether answers are correct, but pushes students to examine whether answers make sense.
"Ours is the same as Brittany and Patricia's," Wesley said, "but we used words."

"We had one like Matthew and Irene," Keith added, "but it wasn't finished."

"I think they're all the same," Aaron said, "just different ways."

Lynne responded, "That would mean that one-half of a sixth is the same as one-twelfth. Does that make sense?"

Truc was clear about this. "If you made 12 pieces and put them in 2s, then you would have 6 of them. So they're the same."

Lynne knew that not all of the children followed Truc's reasoning, but they suspected he was right since he is a strong math student. Lynne didn't push for having each child understand all the fractional notations. However, she feels that a discussion like this is useful for all students. Those who get the chance to verbalize their understanding are confirmed; others have the chance to think about something that is new to them.

NOTE At this age, partial understanding of fractions is common. While some children seem to see how the notation makes sense, others are not even interested in thinking about fractional parts.

Kyle and Truc were the only children in the class not distracted by the lines that divided each candy bar into six squares.

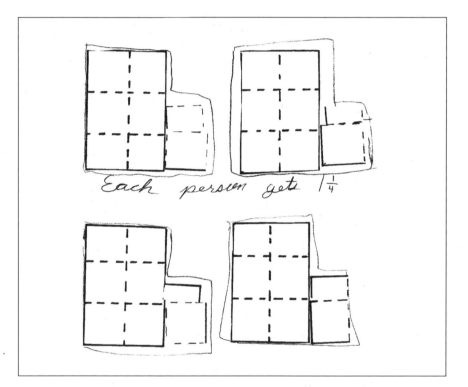

ASSESSMENT   Four Ways to Solve 21 ÷ 4

FROM THE CLASSROOM

Throughout the unit, children confront division problems with remainders and learn to represent the remainders in ways that relate to the contexts of the situations. In this assessment, children are asked to solve one numerical problem—21 ÷ 4—in different contexts. In each case, they record their answers symbolically and draw pictures to show how they figured.

To present the assessment, write the numerical problem in two ways on the board:

$$21 \div 4 = \ 4\overline{)21}$$

Tell the children that they will solve the same problem in four different ways. Write on the board:

1. Divide 21 balloons among 4 people.
2. Divide 21 cookies among 4 people.
3. Divide $21.00 among 4 people.
4. Do 21 ÷ 4 on a calculator.

Also tell the children that they are to write a division sentence that shows each problem and its answer and draw a picture that explains how they figured it out.

Lynne wrote *21 ÷ 4* on the board and said to the class, "You've been solving many problems like this one. Today, however, you'll solve this one problem in four different ways." She then wrote the four statements on the board.

As Lynne wrote, some of the children began to talk with one another about the problems.

"You'd have leftover balloons," Cynthia said.

"Oooh, cookies again. I like cookies," Justine said.

"Not me," Matthew said, "unless they're real cookies."

"I think they're hard," Veronica said, watching Lynne write the problems.

"Nah, they're not so bad," said Aaron.

When she had finished writing on the board, Lynne explained to the children what they were to do. "For each problem," she said, "you should write a division sentence that shows your answer in a way that makes sense. And you should also draw a picture that shows me how you thought about solving it." She then added a final direction. "I'd like you to work alone on this," she said. "That will help me know how each of you thinks about problems like these."

Irene's work was typical of those children who understand that leftovers in different real-world situations require different solutions. She let one balloon fly off, divided the extra cookie into fourths, and exchanged the leftover dollar for quarters.

Irene showed her ability to represent division problems pictorially and numerically.

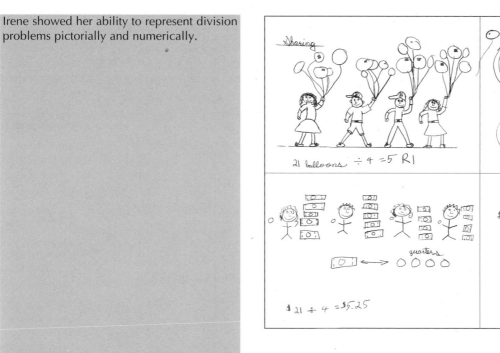

Courtney showed that she understood the fractional notation for one-fourth. To interpret the calculator answer, she wrote: *The 5 is how many in each group. The point means there's a R something. The 25 means theres ¹/₄ left.*

Courtney was explicit in her interpretation of the calculator answer.

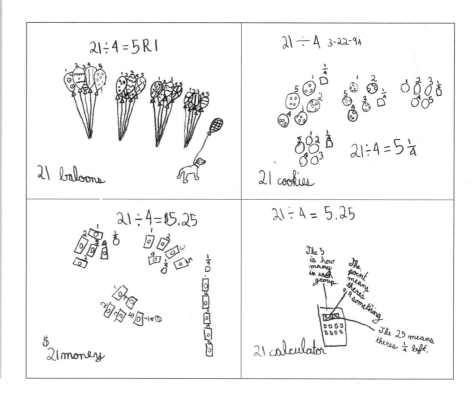

Ethan related the calculator answer to the real-life contexts of cookies and pizza.

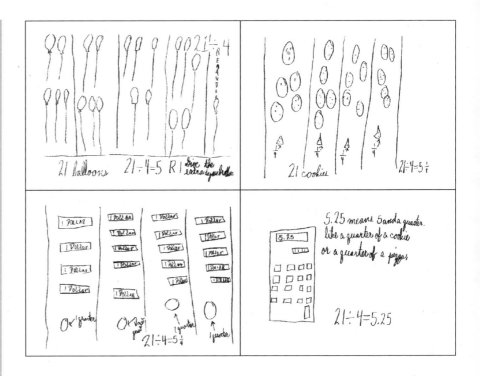

Ethan also understood fractional notation. He interpreted the calculator answer in terms of dividing cookies and pizza.

More than half of the class exhibited the level of understanding that Irene, Courtney, and Ethan did.

The remaining children typically showed that they could represent the situation pictorially, but they either got the wrong answer, didn't use conventional symbolism to record their answers, or used the symbolism incorrectly.

On Kent's paper, for example, the illustrations made sense, but either he didn't record the division sentence or, as with the cookie problem, he used incorrect notation. (Kent's work appears on the facing page.)

Vivian saw that all the answers were the same and wrote *5R1* for each solution. She didn't see that the leftover dollar could be divided into quarters. She entered the problem on the calculator, got "5.25," and "translated" this into 5R1. She even drew a calculator (eight times) with *5R1* on the display screen. (Vivian's work appears on the facing page.)

A few children had extreme difficulty and solved only one or two of the problems, or did a little on each one but weren't able to complete any.

Hugh, for example, divided the balloons into groups of four. Although his picture showed 1 balloon left over, he wrote: *They each have 5*, without mentioning a remainder. Hugh didn't find a relationship between four kids sharing 21 balloons and four kids sharing 21 cookies. He thought they would get 5 balloons each but only 4 cookies each, with 5 cookies left over.

Hugh also misunderstood the point of the calculator problem. Suddenly he had 21 children and 4 calculators. His solution was: *17 kids didn't get a calculator.* For his solution to the money problem, he referred to his solution for the calculator problem. He drew 21 dollar bills and 4 children, gave each child a dollar, and wrote: *17 where left over agin.*

Kent didn't demonstrate an ability to use division notation.

Vivian used only the "R1" form of representing remainders.

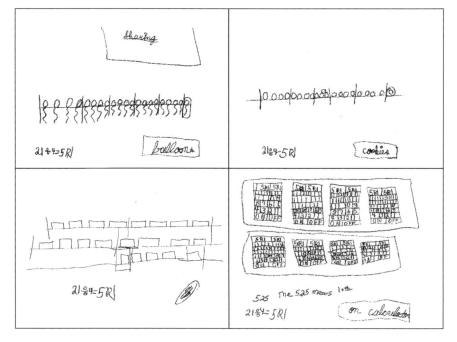

Carey made sense pictorially of the balloon problem, drawing balloons in four groups and showing the leftover, but he ignored the extra in his answer. He did the same for the money and cookie problems, showing remainders but not recording them. He didn't do the calculator problem.

When we examine the children's work closely, we see more and more possible interpretations. Maybe Vivian's leaving a $1.00 remainder

doesn't mean she didn't know she could split it up; maybe she didn't *want* to split it up. Vivian didn't say what she would do with the leftover, but other children were explicit. Aaron, one of the most able students, said he'd give each person $5.00 and put the remainder in his parents' bank account. Other children gave the leftover dollar to Dad, to the poor, or to the youngest child. Amari recommended: *Send it away.*

There was considerable evidence that the children were learning from one another, trying other students' approaches. Keith, for example, was taken with Wesley's system of lines showing who got which part in equal sharing. (See page 134.) Although Wesley did not employ that method on this problem, Keith did. When he shared his work, children noticed and remembered this problem-solving style, saying "Keith did it like Wesley."

MENU ACTIVITY

Overview

Hungry Ants

One Hundred Hungry Ants, written by Elinor J. Pinczes, tells the story of 100 ants hurrying to sample the food at a nearby picnic. The book entertains children and adds to their understanding of division through examining rectangular arrays. For the menu activity, children work individually to explore how to group other numbers of ants.

206

Hungry Ants   I

1. Figure out what would happen if 20 ants tried to group themselves into 1 line, 2 lines, 3 lines, and so on up to 10 lines. How many ants would be in each line?

   Record your answers like this:

   ### 20 Hungry Ants

     1 line of _____
     2 lines of _____
     3 lines of _____
     4 lines of _____
     5 lines of _____
     6 lines of _____
     7 lines of _____
     8 lines of _____
     9 lines of _____
   10 lines of _____

2. Choose another number of ants and do the activity again.

From *Math By All Means: Division, Grades 3–4* ©1995 Math Solutions Publications

Before the lesson

Gather these materials:
■ *One Hundred Hungry Ants* by Elinor J. Pinczes (See Children's Books section, page 186.)
■ Blackline master of menu activity, page 206

Getting started

■ Read the story aloud to the class. In the story, one enterprising ant decides that marching to the picnic in single file is too slow and suggests that the ants regroup into 2 lines of 50, then into 4 lines of 25, 5 lines of 20, and finally into 10 lines of 10. However, by the time the ants arrive at the picnic, all the food is gone.

■ Reread the story or have a class discussion in which the children retell what happened. This time, have children figure out how many ants were in each line whenever the ants regrouped.

■ Show the children how rectangular arrays connect to division by using division symbolism to record how to represent each way the ants regrouped:

$$100 \div 2 = 50 \qquad 2\overline{)100}\,^{50}$$

$$100 \div 4 = 25 \qquad 4\overline{)100}\,^{25}$$

$$100 \div 5 = 20 \qquad 5\overline{)100}\,^{20}$$

$$100 \div 10 = 10 \qquad 10\overline{)100}\,^{10}$$

■ Raise the question: Why didn't the littlest ant tell the other ants to get into three lines? Have the children figure out how many ants would be in each line and how many extras there would be. Talking with the children about how they would write the answer gives you another opportunity to talk about representing remainders: $100 \div 3 = 33$ R1.

■ Explain the menu activity to the children. Tell them they are to work individually on the two parts of the activity:

1. Students figure out what would happen if 20 ants tried to group themselves into 1 line, 2 lines, 3 lines, and so on up to 10 lines.

2. Then the students choose any other number they'd like and repeat the activity. Having children choose their own numbers gives you an idea of their numerical comfort levels.

■ After all students have had a chance to complete the activity, initiate a class discussion. Ask volunteers to present their work and explain how they figured the answers.

FROM THE CLASSROOM

Lynne gathered the class at the front of the room and read the story aloud. The children were fascinated and delighted by it. There was some discussion about the plight of the littlest ant.

"He's really in trouble," Matthew said.

"They're going to get him," Courtney said, "but I don't think that's fair. They would've been late anyway."

"They didn't even see the animals taking food!" Reggie exclaimed. He had noticed the illustrations of other animals carrying food.

"He's really in trouble," Matthew repeated.

"How did the ants start out?" Lynne asked to focus the children on the rectangular arrays in the story.

"In one line of 100," Brittany answered. Lynne wrote on the board:

1 line of 100

"What did the littlest ant do first?" Lynne asked.

"He put them in two lines," Wesley answered.

"There were 50 in each line," Tano added.

Lynne wrote on the board:

2 lines of 50

Ethan raised his hand to report what came next. "Then they went into four lines of 25," he said. Lynne recorded:

4 lines of 25

About a third of the students raised their hands to report what happened next. Lynne called on Amari.

"Next came five lines with . . . ," she faltered, and began to count out loud by 5s. That didn't seem to help her.

"It's 20," Aaron said. Amari looked up at Lynne.

"Aaron's right," Lynne confirmed and wrote on the board:

5 lines of 20

"Let's count by 20s to 100," she said. The children counted aloud with her as she wrote on the board. "So there are five 20s in 100," she said.

Lynne then took the time to draw Xs on the board in five lines of 20 each.

```
x x x x x x x x x x x x x x x x x x x x
x x x x x x x x x x x x x x x x x x x x
x x x x x x x x x x x x x x x x x x x x
x x x x x x x x x x x x x x x x x x x x
x x x x x x x x x x x x x x x x x x x x
```

Even though this was time-consuming, Lynne thought it would help children who might be confused. She counted aloud by 20s again, this time pointing to each line of 20 Xs as she counted. Then she said to Amari, "If we count by 5s, then you'll get to 100 also, but you'll have to count each row of ants. Let's try it." As the children counted by 5s, Lynne pointed.

"What's the last way the ants reorganized?" Lynne asked. Irene reported and Lynne recorded:

10 lines of 10

"Let me show you how else to record each way the ants lined up," Lynne said, and she recorded on the board:

$$100 \div 2 = 50 \qquad 2\overline{)100}^{\,50}$$

$$100 \div 4 = 25 \qquad 4\overline{)100}^{\,25}$$

$$100 \div 5 = 20 \qquad 5\overline{)100}^{\,20}$$

$$100 \div 10 = 10 \qquad 10\overline{)100}^{\,10}$$

Lynne then posed a problem. "Why didn't the littlest ant put them into three lines?" Some children raised their hands, immediately knowing that putting the ants in three lines would leave one left over; others, however, did not know this. "Talk to your neighbor," Lynne said, "and compare what you think."

After a few minutes, Lynne asked the children for their attention. She called on Justine.

"It doesn't work," said Justine. "There would be three lines with 33 in each, and an extra ant." Lynne wrote on the board:

3 lines of 33 R1

Reggie reported what he and Keith had discussed. "We thought that the extra ant could be like the leader," he said.

"Yeah, it could be the littlest ant," Brenna added.

Lynne then presented the menu activity. "In this activity, you pretend that 20 ants were going to the picnic in one long line. Then figure out what would happen if the ants reorganized into 2 lines, then 3, 4, and so on up to 10." Lynne wrote on the board:

20 Hungry Ants
1 line of 20
2 lines
3 lines
4 lines
5 lines
6 lines
7 lines
8 lines
9 lines
10 lines

"Set up your paper like this," she said. "For some lines, there will be extra ants, so you can record the answer the way I did for 100 ants in three lines.

"When you've done this for 20 ants, then do it again, but this time for any number of ants that you choose. Set up your paper the same way, but change the 20 in the title to the number you choose."

There were no questions, so Lynne let the children go to work on the menu.

Observing the Children

The children worked in different ways. Some set up their papers as Lynne had shown on the board and then worked on each example in order. Others skipped around, doing what they knew first. Some children drew diagrams to see what happened when the ants got into different numbers of rows; some used materials such as beans or tiles; others figured in their heads or calculated on paper.

Matthew was using a calculator. "How does the calculator help you?" Lynne asked him.

"I've got this system," he said. "See, I do division, and if I get a weird number, then I do times."

"Show me what you mean," Lynne said. Several other children overheard and gathered around. Matthew enjoyed the attention.

"See, with six lines, I pressed 20 divided by 6." Matthew pushed the buttons and showed Lynne the answer: 3.3333333. "So, I know it doesn't work, but I know they can go in three lines, so I do times, like this." He pressed 3 × 6 and got 18. "So there are two extras."

"Neat!" Aaron said, appreciating Matthew's reasoning.

"I'm going to do that," Ethan said.

"I don't get it," Carey complained. "I like to draw better."

Calie came to show Lynne her work in progress. "Look," she said, "I filled in 1, 2, 4, and 5. I know those work." She had put a star next to each. Her finished paper showed that she also found that putting the ants into 10 lines came out even.

"How did you figure these out?" Lynne asked.

"You mean the ones I didn't already know?" Calie asked. Lynne nodded.

"I used tiles," she explained.

Calie drew stars to indicate lines that had no leftovers.

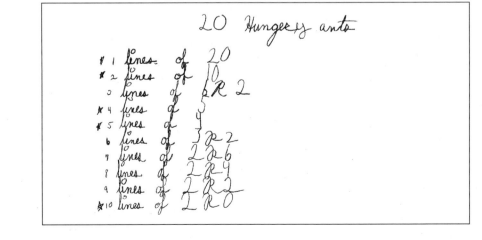

"Our paper's different," Irene said, showing the paper she was working on with Cynthia. "Is this okay?" In the corner of their paper, they had drawn a picnic tablecloth. They made diagrams, found six ways for the ants to line up, and used multiplication to record them: *1 × 20, 2 × 10, 4 × 5, 20 × 1, 10 × 2, 5 × 4*. Then they wrote: *Here are the ways that the hungry ants can't go to the picnic evenly.* They used division sentences, such as 20 ÷ 6 = 3 R2, to record them. Even though they hadn't worked individually or set up their paper in the way Lynne had requested, their work was thoughtful and correct.

Irene and Cynthia used multiplication and division symbolism to explain their answers.

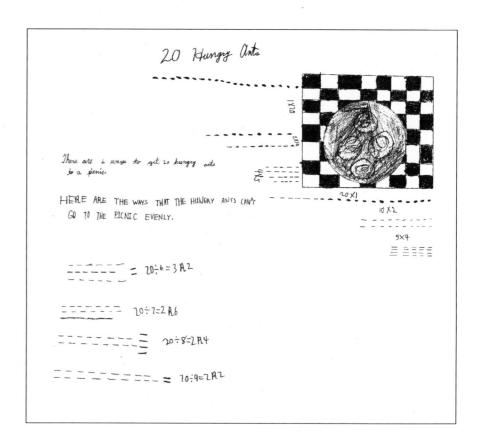

"It's fine," Lynne said. "But when you do the second part, each of you should do your own paper and set it up the way I did."

"Okay," the girls said, and returned to their seats. For the second part of the task Cynthia used 15, and Irene chose 40.

The students' choices of numbers for the second part of the activity ranged from 10 to 80. Gabrielle chose the 80 ants. Lynne noticed that her answers for putting 80 ants in 3, 6, and 7 lines were incorrect. For these numbers, Gabrielle had recorded:

3 lines of 20 R20
10 lines of 6 R20
7 lines of 10 R10

"Show me how you figured this out," Lynne said to her, pointing to her answer for three lines.

"I know 20 times 3 is 60, so that leaves 20," Gabrielle answered.

"Can you draw a picture of ants in three lines with 20 in each?" Lynne asked.

"Sure," Gabrielle said, and drew three rows of circles with 20 in each.

"And the extras?" Lynne asked.

"Okay," Gabrielle said, and began to draw 20 more circles.

"Wait a minute," Lynne interrupted her after she had drawn about 10 circles. "How come those ants aren't getting in line with the others?"

Gabrielle was silent for a minute. Then she said, "Oh, no, my *R* number is too many." She went back to work and corrected the answers, making drawings to check herself. At the bottom of her paper, she wrote: *When my R is too many I just make another line.*

Gabrielle made a discovery about the size of remainders.

80 hungry ants

1 line of 80
2 lines of 40
3 lines of 26 R 2
4 lines of 20
5 lines of 16
6 lines of 13 R 2
7 lines of 11 R 3
8 lines of 10
9 lines of 8 R 8
10 lines of 8

When my R is too many I just make another line.

A Class Discussion

After all the students had completed the menu activity, Lynne initiated a class discussion. She first asked the students to explain how they solved the problem of grouping 20 ants. Then she had volunteers present the work they had done for the second part of the activity.

Wesley explained how he analyzed 18. He had carefully drawn a row of 18 ants to illustrate his first answer. "It took too long," he explained, "so I just did circles."

Wesley chose 18 ants and illustrated each arrangement.

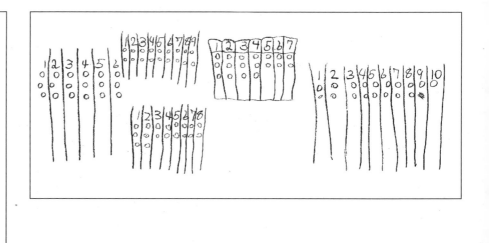

"I did 18, too," Vivian volunteered next, "but my drawings look different." She showed her work. "And I only drew when I couldn't figure it out in my head," she added.

Courtney had chosen 42. She showed her paper and explained how she figured her answers. "I counted up in my head, like 5, 10, 15, 20, 25, 30, 35, 40," she said. She kept track with her fingers as she counted. "When I got to 40, there were 2 left over, so I knew it was 8 remainder 2. Sometimes, I wrote the numbers down."

Vivian used diagrams only when she couldn't figure out the answer in her head.

18 Hungry Ants

1 Line of 18
2 Lines of 9
3 Lines of 6
4 Lines of 4 R2
5 Lines of 3 R3
6 Lines of 3
7 Lines of 2 R4
8 Lines of 2 R2
9 Lines of 2
10 Lines of 1 R8

Courtney wrote the multiples for numbers she didn't automatically know.

42 Hungery Ants
1 lines of 42
2 lines of 21
3 lines of 14
4 lines of 10 R2
5 lines of 8 R2
6 lines of 7
7 lines of 6
8 lines of 5 R2
9 lines of 4 R6
10 lines of 4 R2

4 8 12 16 20 24 28 32 36 40
8 16 24 32 40 48 56
9 18 27 36 45

I counted up. exsample!
5 10 15 20 25 30 35 40
I got to 40 and there
were 2 left over

Ethan had chosen 25 and explained that it was easy to do. "I used my basic facts," he said.

Ethan found 25 easy to do because he knew the multiplication facts.

25 Hungry Ants
1 line of 25
2 lines of 12 R 2
3 lines of 8 R 2
4 lines of 6 R 2
5 lines of 5
6 lines of 4 R 2
7 lines of 3 R 4
8 lines of 3 R 2
9 lines of 2 R 7
10 lines of 2 R 5

I knew my basic facts so this was easy

"I had a hard one to do," Samantha said when it was her turn. "I did 17."

"That's not so big," Matthew commented.

"But it never came out even," Samantha retorted, "except for one line." The others were interested, and Samantha showed her paper. She was one of only four children who had used this standard method for dividing, and Lynne took the opportunity to show the class how it connected to the problem. She wrote one of Samantha's examples on the board and pointed to each number, explaining how it made sense in the context of ants lining up.

$$3\overline{)17} \quad \begin{array}{r} 5 \text{ R2} \\ \hline 17 \\ \underline{15} \\ 2 \end{array}$$

"If you divide 17 ants into three lines," Lynne said, "then there are 5 ants in each line, and that uses up 15 ants. If you subtract 15 from 17, you learn that there are 2 ants left over, so the remainder is 2."

"Look, they all have remainders," Justine said.

"When a number can't be divided evenly by anything except by 1 and itself, it's called *prime*," Lynne said. "Did anyone else pick a prime number?" No one else had.

Samantha chose a prime number and had remainders for all but the first answer.

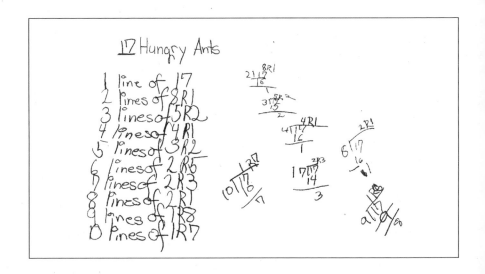

"Does anyone have an idea about other numbers that might work like Samantha's did, with all remainders?"

"Maybe like a million or something," Kent said. "Something big."

"But 1 million ants could get into two lines," Lynne said, "with half a million in each." The class was quiet. Some were thinking about Lynne's question, but others weren't interested in the challenge. Lynne didn't push it. It seemed like a good time to end the class discussion.

A little while later, Aaron came to Lynne. "It would have to be odd," he said.

"What would have to be odd?" Lynne asked, not clear about what Aaron was referring to.

"Well, with an even number of ants, they could always go in two lines," he said. He wandered off, still thinking.

MENU ACTIVITY

Overview

Division Stories

Having children write division stories tells you if they can describe a situation that involves division and if they can relate division to the world around them. Present this menu activity after the children have worked with the mathematical symbols for division and have worked with problems that connect division to real-world situations.

207

Division Stories   I

1. Write a story that meets two conditions:
   a. The story ends with a question.
   b. The question can be answered by dividing.

2. Write the division sentence and figure out the answer. Explain in as many ways as you can how you got your answer.

Before the lesson

Gather these materials:
■ Blackline master of menu activity, page 207

Getting started

■ Review with the children some of the division problems they have solved so far.

■ Tell the class that each student is to write a division story that meets two conditions:

  1. The story ends with a question.
  2. The question can be answered by dividing.

Instruct the children to write the division statement and answer and also to explain how they arrived at their answer. Tell them they may illustrate their stories if they like.

FROM THE CLASSROOM

Lynne introduced this menu activity fairly late in the division unit. She wanted the children to have a variety of experiences involving division and its notation before she asked them to write stories of their own. She looked at the children's stories for evidence that the children were able to connect division with real-world contexts.

"You've been solving many different division problems," Lynne said to introduce the activity. She reviewed a few of the problems the children had solved: dividing cookies, sharing raisins, sharing money, figuring out how 17 kings could take care of 42 elephants, dividing the class into different size groups.

"Now I'd like each of you to write a division story that has two features," Lynne continued. She showed them the menu activity directions, which explained the criteria for the stories. "The story ends with a question, and the question can be answered by dividing," she explained.

"Can we write about cookies?" Brittany wanted to know.

"Yes, you may write about anything that interests you," Lynne responded.

"Can we do an ocean story?" Aaron asked. The class had been working on an oceans unit and were learning about creatures that live in the sea.

"Yes," answered Lynne.

There were no other questions, so Lynne gave one further direction. "Write the division mathematically, find the answer, and be sure to explain your reasoning. Put your answer on the back of your paper."

Observing the Children

Lynne needed to troubleshoot several problems as the students worked on their division stories. Some of the stories didn't pose a division problem. For example, Demetrius wrote: *There were 75 trolls 26 got eaten by 2 lions. How many trolls were still alive?*

"How would you solve that problem?" Lynne asked him.

Demetrius read the problem to himself and saw its flaw immediately. "I'd have to subtract," he said. "I know how to fix it." He added: *If there were 2 lions, how many did they eat the same amount?*

Demetrius's last sentence made his first story a division problem.

When he turned in his paper, Demetrius had written the answer without a division sentence. "You need to write a division sentence to show how your story is about division, and you also need to explain how you got your answer." Lynne told him. Demetrius went back to work. Lynne felt comfortable pushing Demetrius.

Demetrius decided to start all over again with a new story: *15 dogs were climbing a mountain. They had 60 doggie treats. How many doggie treats would each dog get?* This time, he explained his answer with words, pictures, and represented it symbolically in two ways.

In his second story, Demetrius explained his solution several ways.

Some children didn't end their stories with questions. For example, Justine wrote: *I saw 1 dollar on the floor. I shared it with my friend beth and we got 50c each. We bought gum.*

Justine's first story didn't end with a question.

Justine had entered the class at the beginning of the division unit and reported that she "did a lot of workbooks" at her previous school. She works hard and is anxious to complete tasks. Lynne pointed out to Justine that her story needed to end with a question, so there would be a division problem to solve.

"What do you mean?" Justine asked, eager to do well.

"Well, you figured out that you and your friend Beth got 50 cents each," Lynne explained. "Instead of telling how much you both got, you should end the story by asking the question about how much went to each of you."

"Okay," Justine said. When she handed in her story later, Justine had written a completely new situation. This time, however, her story presented a multiplication problem: *There were 19 pairs of shoes how many laces in all.* Justine used both division and multiplication to represent the situation. Describing division correctly poses a difficult language problem for some children.

Justine's second problem was a multiplication situation; however, she symbolically showed the connection between multiplication and division.

As they worked on writing their stories, some students wrote complicated problems that involved several operations. For example, Irene wrote an ocean story: *If there were 50 sharks and they found 250 fish and 10 were scared away then 15 more were scared. How many would be eaten? How many would be left over?* Her solution showed that she understood she needed to subtract before dividing.

Irene's problem called for subtracting first and then dividing.

A Sharing Story

250 If there were 50 sharks and they found fish and 10 were scared away then 15 more were scared. How many would be eaten? How many would be left over?

Solutions: 250-10=240-15=225 50)225 -200 25 (4)

Samantha wrote a long and involved ocean story about sea otters with babies that grew up. The eventual problem was that 100 sea otters caught 150 fish and tried to divide them equally. She solved the problem by herself and also by using a calculator.

Samantha's long story presented the problem 150 ÷ 100.

A Sharing Story

There were 10 sea otters. Each of them had 1 baby. They were all best friends, so they shared the responsibility of each little baby otter. The little otters were not little for long. Soon they had grown up and had babies for their own. The sea otters mother sometimes took care of their babies babies. One sea otter holiday the sea otters went out to caitch a bunch of fish for the feast that night. Now, there were 100 sea otters and they caught 150 fish. How would they ÷ them up equley.

100 fish   100 otter
150=100+50   1 fish for each otter
1 ½   50 is half of 100
1   so it would be 1½
150 ÷100 = 1.5 (on the calculator)
1 means 1whole And the 5 means 1 half.

Ethan's ocean story was about great white sharks and their victim scuba divers. He wrote: *60 scuba divers became the victims of 8 great white sharks. If the sharks shared the scuba divers equally how many would they get?*

Ethan's ocean story was about great white sharks and scuba divers.

As usual, Courtney included cats in her story. She wrote: *9 cats went to the candy shop and bought 99 licorice sticks how many licorice sticks did each cat get?* Her work showed that she saw the relationship between division and multiplication.

Courtney's solution explained her thinking process.

Jamie's story was also about cats. She posed a division problem that included extraneous information. She wrote: *There were 13 cats and 13 bugs. Each cat put 2 drops of butter on a bug. How many bugs did each cat get?*

When Lynne asked her about the two drops of butter, Jamie wrote an explanation that added a reference to multiplication: *There were 26 drops of butter in all.*

In her story, Jamie included a reference to multiplication.

A Class Discussion

Lynne invited the children to share their stories with one another, and about a third of the children were interested in reading their stories aloud. However, the class discussion wasn't a long one. Instead, Lynne put the children's work in a folder and encouraged the children to read one another's problems.

Lynne commented on the students' stories. "Their stories reveal the numbers they're comfortable with," she said, "and their ability to use language to describe division situations."

ASSESSMENT Explaining 13 ÷ 4 = 3 R1

This assessment is similar to *What Is 20 ÷ 4?* (see page 105), but asks students to explain a division problem that has a remainder. To introduce the assignment, write on the board:

$$13 \div 4 = 3 \text{ R1}$$

Tell the students to imagine that a boy named Billy didn't understand this problem. (Be sure *not* to choose the name of someone in the class!) Ask the students to think about how they would explain 13 ÷ 4 = 3 R1 to Billy.
Write on the board:

What would you tell Billy to help him
understand the problem?

"Before you go to work on the menu," Lynne said to the class, "I'd like you to do some writing about a problem." She wrote on the board:

$$13 \div 4 = 3 \text{ R1}$$

"Imagine that a new boy named Billy came to our class, and he hadn't learned about division yet," Lynne continued. "Think about how you could help Billy understand the problem and the answer. Then write about what you might tell him." She wrote on the board:

What would you tell Billy to help him
understand the problem?

"Can we work together?" Brittany asked.
Courtney answered her. "No, this is the kind of problem where Mrs. Zolli likes to know what we each think." Lynne could hear her own inflection in Courtney's response.
"Yes," Lynne confirmed. "I'd like you to write your own explanation so I can learn about how each of you would explain the problem."
The children began working. They understood the assignment, and almost all of them had an idea about what to do. Lynne circulated as the children wrote.
Ethan set his explanation in a military context and was pleased with his idea. "This is going to be good," he said after he had written part of his explanation. "It's about the air force."
Wesley, meanwhile, had written: *I would tell Billy to make a math story about 13 ÷ 4 = 3 R1 with me.* Wesley was having difficulty deciding what sort of story to write and came over to take a look at what Ethan was writing. "That's neat," he said. "I'm going to write about a general." He returned to his seat and added to his paper: *Story: The General sent out 13 men in groups of 3 the 3 men on each team but there one extra guy he got*

shot so the other 12 blew up the enemy. Wesley was pleased and showed his paper to Lynne.

"Help me understand how each part of 13 ÷ 4 = 3 R1 is in your story," she said.

"The remainder is the guy who got shot," Wesley grinned. "That made the groups even."

"What do you mean?" Lynne probed.

"See, there's three guys on each team, so there was one left over," he answered.

Lynne nodded. "But what about the 4 in the problem?" she asked. "Where does the 4 fit into your story?"

"Oh," Wesley said, "there were four teams." He hesitated. "Do I need to say that?"

"You need to explain all parts of the problem to help Billy understand," Lynne replied. Wesley returned to his seat and added: *The 4 means there are 4 groups.*

Wesley wrote an army story.

At the end of his explanation, Ethan incorporated Wesley's idea about including a general. He wrote: *I would tell him to imagine the airforce that they were going with the group of army but there was 13 men for the airforce team but they had to split up in four helicopters. So 3 men in each helicopter but there was the general left so he went with the front group of helicopters.*

Ethan also explained the problem in the context of an army story.

$$13 \div 4 = 3 \, R1$$

I would tell him to imagine the airforce that they were going with the group of army but there was 13 men for the airforce team but they had to split up in four helicopters. So 3 men in each helicopter but there was the general left, so he went with the front group of helicopters

Lynne encourages students to communicate and share their ideas with one another. What's important to Lynne is that the students make ideas their own and express them in their own words.

Cynthia came to show her paper to Lynne. "I used Leftovers," she said. "I think he'd like to learn that game." She had written a direct communication to Billy. She wrote: *"Billy" listen, 13 ÷ 4 = 3 R1. R means a left over, 3 means the answer. Listen you take four plates, and thirteen tiles so you put each one in four plates and you'll end up with 3 R1.*

Cynthia referred to the game of Leftovers.

$$13 \div 4 = 3 \, R1$$

"Billy" listen, 13 ÷ 4 = 3 R1. R means a left over, 3 means the answer. Listen you take four plates, and thirteen tiles so you put each one in four plates and you'll end up with 3 R1!

Justine placed the problem in the context of sharing pizza slices. She wrote: *The 13 means pizza's groups or what ever. The 4 means how many people or animals. The three is the answer. And R1 means how many left over.* She drew a picture of the shared pizza slices and added at the bottom of her paper: *Share the pizza's with the people fairly. You can give the leftover to your teacher.*

Justine shared 13 pizza slices among 4 people.

Demetrius wrote about sharing cookies. His written explanation was clear: *To understand 13 ÷ 4 = 3 R1, just take 13 cookies. Divide them with 4 people. There would be 1 left over. That is the remainder. Each pile would have 3.* However, Demetrius's drawing showed 12 cookies in three groups of four each, as if the cookies had been divided among three people.

"Show me the cookies that would be one person's share," Lynne asked him.

"Here," Demetrius said, pointing to one group of four.

"And the second person?"

"Here." Demetrius pointed to the middle group, and then pointed to the third group, adding, "This is for the third person."

"But which cookies does the fourth person get?" Lynne asked.

"What do you mean?" Demetrius was confused.

"You wrote that you divide the 13 cookies among four people," Lynne said, "and that makes sense. So I'm asking how your drawing shows what you wrote. It seems to me that you divided the cookies into groups with four cookies in each."

"Is it wrong?" asked Demetrius.

"No," Lynne said. "Your story is right and your picture is right. They're two different ways to explain the problem—four groups of three or three groups of four."

"So it's not wrong?" Demetrius asked. Lynne decided not to push further since Demetrius didn't seem able to see the discrepancy between his two interpretations, and Lynne knew that each was a correct way to interpret 13 ÷ 4. She accepted his paper.

Demetrius used the context of sharing cookies.

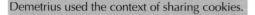

> 13 ÷ 4 = 3 R1
>
> To understand 13÷3 R1, just take 13 cookies. Divide them with 4 people. There would be 1 left over. That is the remainder. Each pile would have 3.

Aaron's paper was unique in that he related the division to multiplication. He wrote: *If Billy knows times then he would know division much easier. If he does not know what R1 is then I would say it means 1 leftover. If he knows times then 3 × 4 = 12 R1.* Aaron represented his thinking two ways, by writing *3 6 9 12 R1* and by picturing four groups with three circles in each and a remainder of 1.

Aaron related division to multiplication.

> 13 ÷ 4 = 3 R1
>
> 3 6 9 12 R1
>
> If Billy knows times then he would know division much easyer. If he does not know what R1 is then I would say it means 1 left over. If he knows times then 3 x 4 = 12 R1.

Brenna shared flowers and put them into three groups of four as Demetrius had with cookies. She wrote: *In the problem 13 ÷ 4 = 3 R1 the 13 is the number you start out with then you take the number 4 and put it into 13 as many times as you can. You can put it in 3 times but you still have 1 left over and that's the R1.* She drew 13 flowers, and numbered them 1, 1, 1, 1, 2, 2, 2, 2, 3, 3, 3, 3, and R1.

"How many people got flowers?" Lynne asked, to see how Brenna would explain her picture. Brenna's explanation, however, was consistent with her diagram. She explained further: *All the flowers that have 1 in them go to 1 person the same with 2 and 3 the flower that says R1 is the left over.*

Brenna used flowers to explain how to divide 13 by 4.

13 ÷ 4 = 3 R1

In the problem 13 ÷ 4 = 3 R1 the 13 is the number you start out with then you take the number 4 and put it into 13 as many times as you can. You can put it it in 3 times but you still have 1 left over and thats the R1.

All the flowers that have 1 in them go to 1 person the same with 2 and 3 the flower that says R1 is the left over.

ASSESSMENT

How Are Division and Multiplication Alike?

FROM THE CLASSROOM

The primary focus of this assessment is to find out if children understand how division and multiplication relate to each other. This assessment draws on the same context used for *Explaining 13 ÷ 4 = 3 R1* (see page 174) in which children explained their understanding to "Billy," an imaginary student. For this assignment, the children again explain something to Billy. Tell them: "Someone told Billy that division and multiplication are alike, and someone else told him that division and multiplication aren't alike. Billy wants to know which statement is true or if both of them are true." Ask the children to write about what they would tell Billy. (Again, be sure not to choose the name of someone in your class.)

To introduce this assessment, Lynne reminded the children of the explanations they had written to "Billy" earlier in the unit. "You explained to him what 13 ÷ 4 = 3 R1 meant," Lynne said. "Now I have something else for you to explain to Billy. Listen carefully."

Lynne then presented the situation. "Someone told Billy that division and multiplication are alike," she began. "And someone else told him that division and multiplication aren't alike. Billy is confused. He doesn't know if the first person is right, if the second person is right, or if they both are right. I'd like each of you to write about what you might tell Billy. Explain to him how multiplication and division are alike and how they are different. Include examples to help Billy understand your explanation."

Lynne then wrote on the board:

> Someone told Billy that division and multiplication
> are alike. Someone else told him that division and
> multiplication aren't alike. What would you tell Billy?

Lynne gave one more direction. "When you're finished," she said, "bring your paper to me. Then you can go to work on the menu."

The children began to get organized to write. "This is so easy," Aaron said, beginning to write immediately.

Ashley sat down and then, repeating behavior that had become almost automatic, stood up and went to Lynne for help. This time she asked for help before even writing her name on her paper. Lynne asked her to read the assignment written on the board.

"So I tell Billy which is right?" she asked Lynne.

"Yes," Lynne responded.

"Oh, I get it!" exclaimed Ashley, ever enthusiastic.

Tano, Truc, and Keith took out calculators and began to experiment with numbers.

Amari talked as she wrote, "My cousin is in sixth grade, and she still doesn't know division."

Lynne circled the room, consulting with children about their thinking. She noticed that Hugh had written: *4 × 5 = 20. 20 ÷ 5 is opposite.*

"What does that mean?" she asked.

"The numbers are the same, but they're switched around," he answered.

Vivian approached Lynne on the verge of tears. Lynne spoke softly and matter-of-factly. Along with telling Vivian not to cry, she gave her simple directions she could follow. "Don't cry. Bring your pencil up here. Don't cry."

Vivian gulped back tears and returned to her table to get her pencil. In the beginning of the year, whenever Vivian felt any stress she became hysterical. Lynne noted how far Vivian had come. Learning to struggle with new information, control her tears, and find acceptable ways of getting attention was real progress.

In the meantime, Lynne approached Reggie. He kept repeating, "I don't get it."

Lynne drew five pairs of circles on a piece of paper. "What can you tell me about this?" she asked.

"Two groups of 5; 2 times 5 equals 10," Reggie answered. Lynne wrote:

$$2 \times 5 = 10$$

"What would you say if I told you that you have 10 balloons and five people?"

"Oh!" exclaimed Reggie. "I get it. Multiplication is 2 times 5; division is 10 divided by 2. Or maybe it's 10 divided by 5." Lynne left Reggie to decide what to do next.

Reggie used Lynne's suggestion of two groups of five, then extended it.

Vivian showed how the same illustration can be described by multiplication and division.

Remembering that Vivian had been upset, Lynne looked up to check. She saw Vivian at her desk writing on her paper. She wandered over and noticed that Vivian had drawn a row of 12 circles and divided them into four groups of 3. She had written: *4 × 3 = 12 and 12 ÷ 3 = 4.*

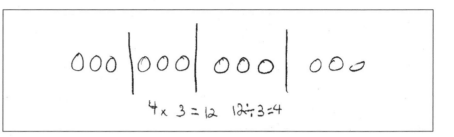

Children began bringing their finished papers to Lynne to check. Throughout the assessment, Lynne had been talking to children, probing, guiding. "I don't mind helping them during an assessment. I want them to learn something from the assessment, and talking to them helps me learn a great deal about how they're thinking."

Some children explained why they thought multiplication and division were both alike and opposites. Ethan wrote: *In some ways × and ÷ are alike and in some ways their not. Their alike because their like opposites. For example 24 ÷ 3 = 8 and when you × 3 × 8 it comes out to be 24. Their not alike because in × the answer gets higher and in ÷ the answer gets lower.*

Ethan saw multiplication and division as opposites.

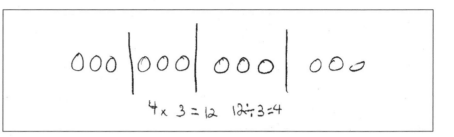

Some children wrote only about how multiplication and division were alike. Jamie wrote: *They are alike because they are both math, and they are both alike because 3 groups of 2 = 6 and 6 ÷ 2 = 3.*

Jamie explained how multiplication and division are alike.

They are alike because they are both math, and they are both alike because 3 groups of 2 = 6 and 6÷2=3.

Several children talked about how multiplication related to addition while division related to subtraction. According to Calie: *× and ÷ can be alike and can't be alike in ways. For example, 6 × 3 = 18 and reversed is 18 ÷ 3 = 6. That's what makes them alike. Another example is ÷ is repeated subtraction and × is repeated addition. Like 18 – 6 = 12 – 6 = 6 – 6 = 0 is also 18 ÷ 6 = 3 and 6 + 6 + 6 = 18 is also 3 × 6 = 18.*

Calie understood that multiplication is repeated addition and division is repeated subtraction.

X and ÷

X and ÷ can be alike and can't be alike in ways. For example, 6×3=18 and reversed is 18÷3=6. That what makes them alike. Another example is ÷ is repeated subtraction and X is repeated addition. Like 18-6=12-6-6-6=0 is also 18÷6=3 and 6+6+6=18 is also 3×6=18.

18÷6=3

3×6=18
6 + 6 + 6 = 18

Some children, Aaron and Irene, for example, drew rectangular arrays to illustrate their ideas.

(right) Aaron showed the relationship between 24 ÷ 3 = 8 and 8 × 3 = 24.

(left) Irene used a rectangular array to support her explanation.

> X and ÷
>
> I would tell Billy that the two people that they were both right Cause division and multiplication are a like and not a like Like if you had a division promblem, like this one 81 ÷ 9 = 9 so if you put 9 × 9 = 81.
>
> If you still don't get it look at the picture below.
>
> 5 × 7 = 35
> and
> 35 ÷ 7 = 5

> X and ÷
>
> I'd tell Billy division and multiplication are alike and different. For example, 24 ÷ 8 = 3 Division and multiplication can be used. To use division you put 24 into 8 pieces and each piece will be 3. To use multiplication use 8 × 3 = 24 because 3, 8's go into 24.
>
> ÷   X   24 ÷ 3 = 8
>
> 3 × 8 = 24
>
> Person 1 Person 2 Person 3

Courtney's response was similar to Jamie's, but it also reflected her feeling about multiplication and division. She wrote: *× and ÷ are alike because there both math. Also they both are hard if you don't partice.*

Courtney's response indicated how she felt about multiplication and division.

> x and ÷ are alike because there both math. Also they both are hard if you don't partice

CONTENTS

The Doorbell Rang   186
One Hundred Hungry Ants   186
17 Kings and 42 Elephants   187

CHILDREN'S BOOKS

Children's picture books have long been one of teachers' favorite tools for nurturing students' imaginations and helping them develop appreciation for language and art. In the same way, children's books that have a connection to mathematics can help students develop an appreciation for mathematical thinking. They can stimulate students to think and reason mathematically and help them experience the wonder possible in mathematical problem solving.

Each of the three children's books described in this section can add a special element to one or more of the activities in the division unit. A synopsis and a reference to an activity in the unit are provided for each book.

The Doorbell Rang
by Pat Hutchins
Greenwillow Books, 1986

In Pat Hutchins's story, Ma has baked a plate of cookies for Victoria and Sam to share. The two children figure out that they each get six cookies, but then the doorbell rings and in walk Tom and Hannah from next door. Just after the four children figure out how to share the cookies, the doorbell rings again and two more children arrive. When the doorbell rings again, six children stand at the door. The doorbell rings one more time, as each of the 12 children stares nervously at his or her one cookie. But it's Grandma at the door, with "an enormous tray of cookies."

"'And no one makes cookies like Grandma,' said Ma as the doorbell rang."

Read this book at the beginning of the whole class lesson *The Doorbell Rang (see page 32)* and, if you like, at the beginning of the menu activity *The Doorbell Rings Again.* (See page 89.)

One Hundred Hungry Ants
by Elinor J. Pinczes
illustrated by Bonnie MacKain
Houghton Mifflin Co., 1993

Elinor J. Pinczes tells the whimsical story of 100 hungry ants setting out in one long line toward a picnic. Then the littlest ant announces:

"We're moving way too slow.
Some food will be long gone
unless we hurry up. So . . .
with 2 lines of 50
we'd get there soon, I know."

The 100 ants follow the littlest ant's advice and stop to form two lines. Later the littlest ant convinces the others to form 4 lines of 25, 5 lines of 20, and 10 lines of 10. By the time they reach the picnic, all the food is gone!

Read this book to introduce the menu activity *Hungry Ants.* (See page 157.)

17 Kings and 42 Elephants
by Margaret Mahy
illustrated by Patricia MacCarthy
Dial Books for Young Readers, 1987

Margaret Mahy takes the reader on a ride through the jungle with 17 kings and 42 elephants. Along the way, they encounter a variety of animals: crocodiles, "hippopotomums," tigers, "baboonsters," and more.

The book has no formal plot, but its appeal comes from the hand-painted illustrations and the way the author uses alliteration, rhythm, and made-up words. An example:

"Tinkling tunesters, twangling trillicans,
Butterflied and fluttered by the great green trees."

Read this book as an introduction to the menu activity of the same name. (See page 135.)

CONTENTS

Dividing with Two People   190
Leftovers   190
A Sharing Problem   191
A Grouping Problem   192

HOMEWORK

Homework assignments help extend children's classroom learning and also inform parents about the kinds of activities their child is doing in school. The mathematics instruction that most parents had differs greatly from the learning experiences in this unit. Homework assignments help parents see what their child has been doing and help them better understand the mathematics instruction their child is receiving.

Four homework assignments are suggested. Two of them, *A Sharing Problem* and *A Grouping Problem,* suggest additional, similar assignments. Each homework assignment is presented in three parts:

Homework directions

The directions explain the assignment and include information, when needed, about what children should do to prepare for the assignment.

The next day

This section gives suggestions for incorporating the students' homework into classroom instruction. It's important for children to know that work they do at home contributes to their classroom learning.

To parents

A note to parents explains the purpose of the homework and ways that they can participate. These communications help parents understand more fully the math instruction their children are getting in school.

HOMEWORK

Dividing with Two People

Give this assignment after the whole class lesson *The Doorbell Rang.* (See page 32.)

Homework directions

Give children several problems in which they have to divide things among two people. Tell them that for each problem, they are to figure out the answer and make a drawing to show their reasoning. This assignment is good at the beginning of the unit when the children are beginning to think about division from a sharing perspective. Following are five suitable problems; duplicate them, or others you think of, for children to take home.

1. Share 25 cents among two people.
2. Share 38 balloons among two people.
3. Share 5 cookies among two people.
4. Share 1 sandwich among two people.
5. Share 13 marbles among two people.

The next day

In small groups, children compare their solutions and show their drawings. Then each group chooses one problem and chooses a spokesperson from the group to present the answer.

To parents

> Dear Parent,
> Learning to share objects is one way of interpreting division in real-world settings. Your child's homework assignment is to solve the five sharing problems on the attached sheet and to draw pictures to illustrate the solutions. Please invite your child to explain how he or she got the answers; your child's thinking is important.

HOMEWORK

Leftovers

Give this assignment after children have had opportunities to play Leftovers in class. (See page 60.)

Homework directions

Ask the students to teach someone at home to play Leftovers. Instead of tiles, they can use pennies, beans, or any small objects. Tell them to bring in their recording sheets from home so they can add new statements to the "Division with R0" class chart. You may want to duplicate the directions for playing Leftovers (see pages 197–198) for the students to take home.

In case students don't have dice at home, show them a substitute. Demonstrate cutting six slips of paper, numbering them from 1 to 6, putting them in a bag, and drawing one out without looking. The number tells them

how many "plates" they take. Remind the students to return the slip of paper to the bag each time before drawing again. Students may want to draw dots on the slips of paper to make them look more like the faces of a die.

The next day

The children report their experiences playing the game at home, telling with whom they played and the responses they got. Ask children to add any new statements to the "Division with R0" class chart.

To parents

> Dear Parent,
> Leftovers is a game of chance that helps children learn about division. The game gives children experience dividing quantities into equal-size groups, thinking about remainders, and recording division statements with standard mathematical symbolism. Please play at least three games with your child.
>   Your child should bring your recording sheet to class so that we can explore those statements that had remainders of zero and also look for patterns in the statements with other remainders.

HOMEWORK

Homework directions

A Sharing Problem

Give children the problem of sharing 54 marbles among two, three, and four people. Ask them to be prepared to talk about their solutions with their classmates and explain their reasoning. (Note: This homework assignment gives children a "sharing" division problem. This type of problem can be repeated by changing the number of marbles—or the objects to money, cubes, or something else—and changing the number of people who will share them.)

The next day

The children talk in small groups about their solutions and their reasoning. Tell them they need to agree on the solution, but they should explore the many different ways there are to figure out the answer. Ask for a volunteer to give the answer and explain his or her thinking. Ask others who reasoned differently to explain their thought processes.

To parents

> Dear Parent,
> One type of division involves sharing objects among a group of people. To help link division with real-world experiences, we have been solving division problems set in a variety of sharing situations. For homework, your child is to solve a sharing problem and explain his or her thinking. In class tomorrow, the children will have a chance to present how they reasoned and hear about how others approached the problem. Class discussions such as these help broaden children's ways of thinking about division.

HOMEWORK

Homework directions

A Grouping Problem

Give students the problem of putting three dozen cookies into picnic boxes so each box has one, two, three, or four cookies. Have the students figure out how many picnic boxes they can fill for each number. (Note: This homework assignment gives students a "grouping" division problem. This type of problem can be repeated by changing the context and the number in each group. For example, students can figure out how many volleyball teams they can make with 3, 4, or 5 on a team if there are 30 players altogether; or, if they have $25.00, how many bunches of flowers they can buy if each bunch costs $3.00, $4,00, or $5.00.)

The next day

The children talk in small groups about their solutions and their reasoning. Tell them they need to agree on the solution, but they should explore the many different ways there are to figure out the answer. Then ask for a volunteer to give the answer and explain his or her thinking. Ask others who reasoned differently to explain their thought processes.

To parents

> Dear Parent,
> One type of division involves grouping objects into equal-size groups. To help link division with real-world experiences, we have been solving division problems set in a variety of grouping situations. For homework, your child is to solve a grouping problem and explain his or her thinking. In class tomorrow, the children will have a chance to present how they reasoned and hear about how others approached the problem. Class discussions such as these help broaden children's ways of thinking about division.

CONTENTS

Division Menu   194
Dividing Cookies (recording sheet)   195
Cookies (worksheet)   196
Directions for Playing Leftovers   197–198
The Doorbell Rings Again   199
Leftovers with Any Number   200
Raisins in the Big Box   201
Candy Box Family Guides   202
17 Kings and 42 Elephants   203
Sharing Candy Bars   204
Candy Bars (worksheet)   205
Hungry Ants   206
Division Stories   207

BLACKLINE MASTERS

The blackline masters fall into several categories:

Division Menu

This blackline master lists the titles of all the menu activities suggested in the unit. You may choose to enlarge and post this list for a class reference. Some teachers fill in the boxes in front of each title once they have introduced the activity so that students know which activities they may choose to do during menu time. Also, some teachers have students copy the list and make check or tally marks each day to indicate the tasks they worked on; other teachers duplicate the blackline master for each student or pair of students.

Menu Activities

Directions for eight menu activities are included. (The directions also appear in the text following the "Overview" section for each menu activity.) You may enlarge and post the menu tasks as you introduce them or make copies for students to use. (Note: A set of classroom posters of the menu activities is available from Cuisenaire Company of America.)

Instructions and Recording Sheets

One blackline master gives the directions for playing Leftovers. Two blackline masters are provided for the *Dividing Cookies* whole class lesson, one with the "cookies" for students to cut out and the other for the students' recording. Another blackline master provides the "candy bars" for the *Sharing Candy Bars* menu activity. Duplicate an ample supply of each of these blackline masters and make them available to students.

Division Menu

☐ The Doorbell Rings Again

☐ Leftovers with Any Number

☐ Raisins in the Big Box

☐ Candy Box Family Guides

☐ 17 Kings and 42 Elephants

☐ Sharing Candy Bars

☐ Hungry Ants

☐ Division Stories

From *Math By All Means: Division, Grades 3–4*   ©1995 Math Solutions Publications

Dividing Cookies

Names _____ _____

_____ _____

Share _____ cookies equally among 4 people.
Paste each person's share in a box.

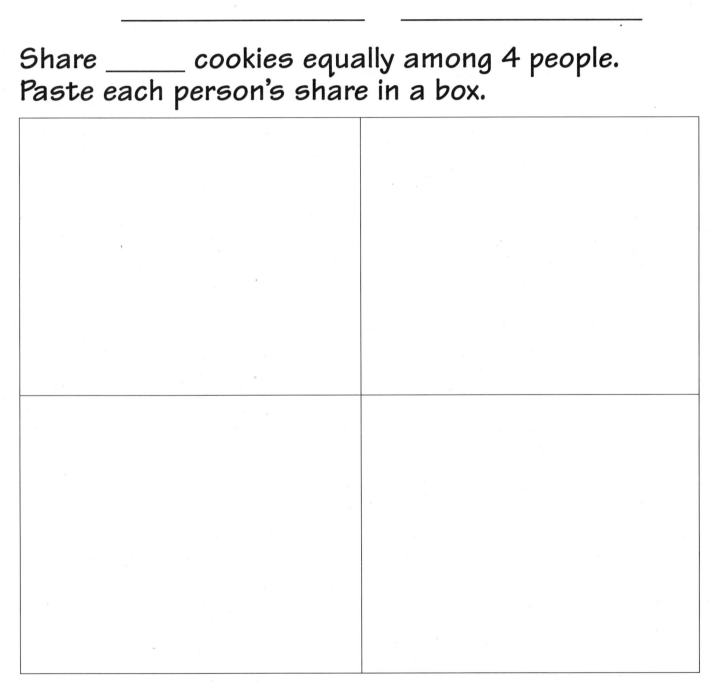

How much did each person get?

From *Math By All Means: Division, Grades 3–4* ©1995 Math Solutions Publications

Cookies

Directions for Playing Leftovers

You need: A partner
             One die
             15 Color Tiles
             One cup to hold the tiles
             Six paper plates or 3-inch paper
             squares ("plates")

1. Take turns. On your turn, roll the die, take that number of paper plates or squares, and divide the tiles among them. Keep any leftover tiles.

2. Both players record the math sentence that describes what happened.

   For example: $15 \div 4 = 3\ R3$

   In front of each sentence write the initial of the person who rolled the die.

3. Return the tiles on the plates to the cup before the next player takes a turn.

From *Math By All Means: Division, Grades 3–4*   ©1995 Math Solutions Publications

Directions for Playing Leftovers (page 2)

4. Play until all the tiles are gone. Then figure your scores by counting how many tiles each of you has. The winner is the player with the most leftovers. Add your scores to make sure that they total the 15 tiles you started with.

5. When you finish a game, look at each of your sentences with a remainder of zero (R0). Write on the class chart each sentence with R0 that isn't already posted.

From *Math By All Means: Division, Grades 3–4* ©1995 Math Solutions Publications

The Doorbell Rings Again $\boxed{\text{I}}$ or $\boxed{\text{P}}$

You need: One sheet of 12-by-18-inch paper

1. Fold the paper into eight sections.

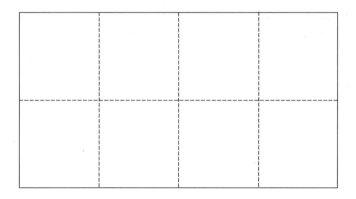

   In the first panel, write "The Doorbell Rings Again" and your name.

2. In the second panel, start your story. Write about some people who are going to divide some things among them. Write a division sentence to show the math problem and then find the answer. Draw a picture to illustrate the problem.

3. In each of the following panels, write about what happens when the doorbell rings. Be sure to write the math problems, find the answers, and draw pictures.

From *Math By All Means: Division, Grades 3–4*   ©1995 Math Solutions Publications

Leftovers with Any Number $\boxed{P}$

You Need: One die
           Color Tiles
           One cup to hold the tiles
           Six paper plates or 3-inch paper
           squares ("plates")

1. Choose how many tiles you want to start with.

2. Play a game of Leftovers.

3. When you finish the game, look at each of your sentences with a remainder of zero (RO). Write on the class chart each sentence with RO that isn't already posted.

From *Math By All Means: Division, Grades 3–4*   ©1995 Math Solutions Publications

Raisins in the Big Box

You need: One 1½-ounce box of raisins

1. Without opening the box, estimate how many raisins are inside. Write your estimate on a sheet of paper.

2. Empty the raisins onto a sheet of paper. Count them. Next to your estimate, write the total number of raisins and explain how you counted them.

3. Divide the raisins among the members of your group. Record how many raisins each person received and explain how you divided them.

From *Math By All Means: Division, Grades 3–4*   ©1995 Math Solutions Publications

Candy Box Family Guides I or P

Prepare a guide that tells different size families what size candy boxes they should buy so that the candy can be shared equally among all members of the family.

The candy cannot be broken into pieces, and there should be no leftover candy.

Make your guide attractive, interesting, and informative.

17 Kings and 42 Elephants   I or P

1. Figure out how many elephants each king gets if the kings share the elephants equally.

2. Explain how you solved the problem. Use words, numbers, and, if you like, pictures.

Sharing Candy Bars

You need: Candy Bars worksheet
Scissors
Glue

1. Figure out how to divide the five "candy bars" equally among four people.

2. Glue the four equal candy parts to a sheet of paper.

3. Explain how much candy each person will get.

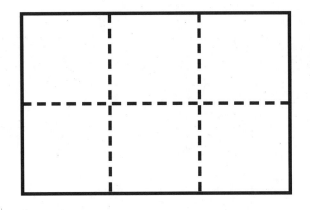

Candy Bars

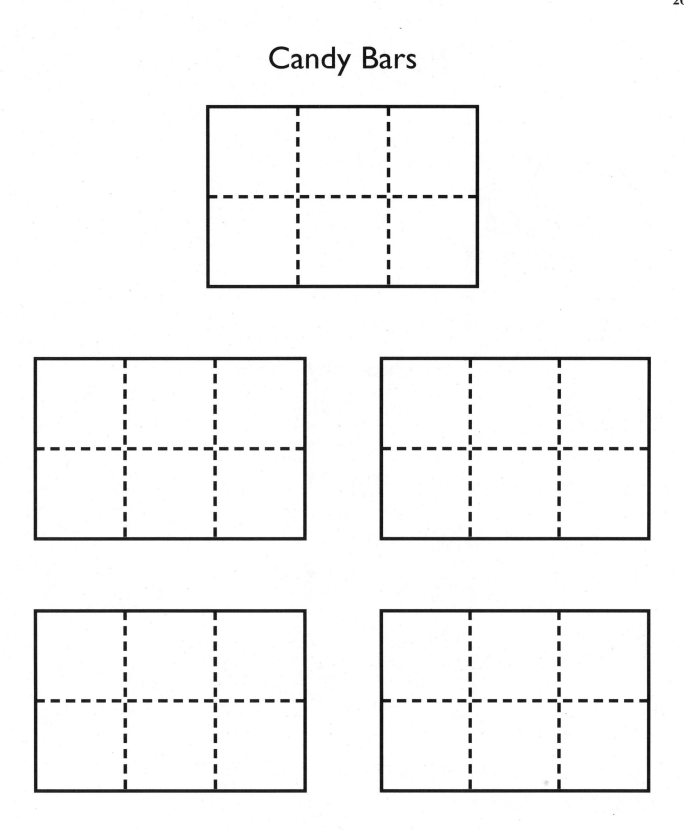

Hungry Ants

1. Figure out what would happen if 20 ants tried to group themselves into 1 line, 2 lines, 3 lines, and so on up to 10 lines. How many ants would be in each line?

   Record your answers like this:

   ### 20 Hungry Ants

1	line of	_____
2	lines of	_____
3	lines of	_____
4	lines of	_____
5	lines of	_____
6	lines of	_____
7	lines of	_____
8	lines of	_____
9	lines of	_____
10	lines of	_____

2. Choose another number of ants and do the activity again.

Division Stories

1. Write a story that meets two conditions:
   a. The story ends with a question.
   b. The question can be answered by dividing.

2. Write the division sentence and figure out the answer. Explain in as many ways as you can how you got your answer.

From *Math By All Means: Division, Grades 3–4*   ©1995 Math Solutions Publications

BIBLIOGRAPHY

Hutchins, Pat. *The Doorbell Rang.* Greenwillow Books, 1986.
Mahy, Margaret. *17 Kings and 42 Elephants.* Dial Books for Young Readers, 1987.
Pinczes, Elinor J. *One Hundred Hungry Ants.* Illustrated by Bonnie MacKain. Houghton Mifflin Co., 1993.

Other Books in the *Math By All Means* Series

Burns, Marilyn. *Math By All Means: Multiplication, Grade 3.* Math Solutions Publications, 1991.
___. *Place Value,* Grades *1–2.* Math Solutions Publications, 1994.
Confer, Chris. *Geometry, Grades 1–2.* Math Solutions Publications, 1994.
Ohanian, Susan, and Marilyn Burns. *Division, Grades 3–4.* Math Solutions Publications, 1995.
Rectanus, Cheryl. *Geometry, Grades 3–4.* Math Solutions Publications, 1994.

Most of these materials are available from: Cuisenaire Co. of America, Inc.
P.O. Box 5026
White Plains, NY 10602-5026
(800) 237-3142

INDEX

Addition, 1, 34

Assessments, 5, 13–14
    Classroom Groups, 125–134
    daily schedule for, suggested, 8–11
    Explaining 13 ÷ 4 = 3 R1, 174–179
    Four Ways to Solve 21 ÷ 4, 152–156
    How Are Division and Multiplication Alike?, 180–184
    What Is Division?, 15–19
    What Is 20 ÷ 4?, 105–108

Bibliography, 209
Blackline masters, 193–207

Calculators, 2, 8, 47–48, 66
    checking answers with, 24, 35, 113, 137, 138
    imperfect understanding of decimals, 1, 41, 42–43, 44, 48, 66, 80, 81, 93, 137, 138
    interpreting 21 ÷ 4 on, 152–155
    use of, 15–16, 24, 41, 48, 80, 81, 82, 112, 161, 180
Candy Box Family Guides, 116-124
Candy Box Research, 116
Children's books, 1, 5, 32–33, 90, 135–136, 157–160, 185–187
Circles, dividing. *See* Dividing Cookies.

Class discussions, 8
    of assessments, 15–16, 125–126, 131–133
    of homework, 189–192
    of menu activities, 99–102, 115, 118, 123–124, 136, 140, 143–144, 150–151, 159–160, 163–164, 166, 173
    of whole class lessons, 28–31, 33–36, 37–38, 45–48, 55–58, 68–70, 78–80
Class lessons. *See* Whole class lessons
Class organization, 5–6
    daily schedule, suggested, 8–11
Classroom Groups, 125–134
Color Tiles, 60–71, 96–104
Cookies, sharing. *See* Dividing Cookies; Doorbell Rang, The; Doorbell Rings Again, The
Cooperation, 5–6

Daily schedule, suggested, 8–11
Decimal points
    explanation of, 41, 48, 137
    not understood, 1, 41, 42–43, 44, 66, 80, 81, 93, 137
    understood, 36, 41, 81, 139, 153–154
Dice
    making, 61, 70, 104, 190–191
    using: *see* Leftovers

Discussions. *See* Class discussions
Dividing Cookies, 49–59, 195, 196
Dividing with Two People, 190
Division
    children's informal knowledge of, 2–3, 15–19
    goal of teaching, 2–3, 13
    symbolism, 2, 15, 32, 34, 105–108
    traditional instruction of, 13
    using correct terminology, 101
Division Stories, 167–173
Divisors, 101, 102
    fractional, 103–104
Doorbell Rang, The, 32–48
Doorbell Rang, The (book), 32, 33, 90, 186, 209
Doorbell Rings Again, The, 89–94

Explaining 13 ÷ 4 = 3 R1, 174–179
Explorations with Raisins, 72–82; *see also* Raisins in the Big Box

Factor, 101
Family sizes, 117, 119
    dividing candy among, 117–124
Folders, 6, 84, 85
Four Ways to Solve 21 ÷ 4, 152–156
Fractions, 40, 48, 50–59, 147–151, 153
    as divisors, 103–104

Game of Leftovers, The, 60–71, 197–198; *see also* Leftovers; Leftovers with Any Number
Grouping, 2, 18, 19, 76–79, 111–114, 125–134, 157–166, 192; *see also* Sharing equally
Grouping Problem, A, 192

Homework, 5, 189–192
    daily schedule for, suggested, 9–11
How Are Division and Multiplication Alike?, 180–184
Hungry Ants, 157–166

Leftovers
    homework, 190–191
    menu activity, 95–104
    whole class lesson, 60–71
Leftovers with Any Number, 95–104

Materials and supplies, 7
Math By All Means, 116, 117, 209
Mathematical notes, 44, 102–104
Menu activities, 4, 6-7
    Candy Box Family Guides, 116–124
    daily schedule for, suggested, 8–11
    Division Stories, 167–173
    Doorbell Rings Again, The, 89–94
    Hungry Ants, 157–166
    introduction to, 83–85
    Leftovers with Any Number, 95–104
    Raisins in the Big Box, 109–115
    recording, 6, 84
    rules, 114

17 Kings and 42 Elephants, 1, 135–144
    Sharing Candy Bars, 145–151
    typical menu day, 85, 87–88
Money, sharing, 22–31
Multiples, 116, 124, 127, 132, 165
Multiplication, 1, 2, 34, 162, 165, 170
    to check division, 104
    as inverse of division, 17, 103, 130, 180–184
    related to division, 180–184

Net weight, 73–74, 115

One Hundred Hungry Ants, 157, 158, 159, 186, 209

Parents
    providing information to, 11–12, 189
    sample letters to, 12, 190–192
Percents, 58
Prime numbers, 166
Proportions, 115

Raisins, 72–82, 109–115
Raisins in the Big Box, 109–115
Range, 73, 80
Remainders, 31, 43, 44, 45, 48
    in Hungry Ants, 158, 160–166
    explaining, 174–179
    in 17 Kings and 42 Elephants, 1, 135–144
    in Leftovers, 60–71, 96–104
    in real-world situations, 152–155

17 Kings and 42 Elephants, 1, 135–144
17 Kings and 42 Elephants (book), 1, 135–136, 187

Sharing, 2
Sharing Candy Bars, 145–151
Sharing equally, 16–19, 51
    candy, 118–124, 146–151
    cookies, 33–59, 90–94
    elephants, 136–144
    money, 22–31
    raisins, 80–82, 113–114
    various things, 90–94
Sharing Money, 22–31
Sharing Problem, A, 191–192
Subtraction, 1, 100

Terminology, using correct, 101

Unit schedule, suggested, 8–11

What Is Division?, 15–19
What Is 20 ÷ 4?, 105–108
Whole class discussions. *See* Class discussions
Whole class lessons, 4, 21
    daily schedule for, suggested, 8–10
    Dividing Cookies, 49–59
    Doorbell Rang, The, 32–48
    Explorations with Raisins, 72–82
    Game of Leftovers, The, 60–71
    group work in, 22–28, 52–55, 80–82
    Sharing Money, 22–31
Writing, 7; *see also* specific assessments; menu activities; whole class lessons

Zero, dividing by, 102–104